To Aunt Ruby,

God bless you.
Much love,
Rhen C. Bast II
7-13-06

ALPHA KAPPA ALPHA SORORITY, INCORPORATED
PRESENTS

The Spirit Within

VOICES of YOUNG AUTHORS

Volume 2

Edited and designed by Creative Curriculum Initiatives

General Editor: Jason Powe
Editor: Judy Rosenbaum
Art DIrector: Debrah Welling
Designers: Christine Kwasnik, Robert Steimle
Cover Designer: Caroline Cox

Photographs:
Cover: Background, Siede Preis/Getty Images, Inc; Upper left, Tom Stewart/CORBIS; Center, Mitch Kezar/Getty Images, Inc; Pages 62–67 and 118–121: PhotoDisc® Volumes: Nature Scenes 36

Copyright © 2006 Alpha Kappa Alpha Sorority, Incorporated.
Published by Alpha Kappa Alpha Sorority, Incorporated. All rights reserved. No part of this work may be reproduced, transmitted, or utilized in any form or by any means, electronic, mechanical, or otherwise, including photocopying and recording, or by any storage and retrieval system, without prior written permission from Alpha Kappa Alpha Sorority, Incorporated.

Alpha Kappa Alpha Sorority, Incorporated
Corporate Office
5656 S. Stony Island Avenue, Chicago, Illinois 60637

ISBN 0-9786500-0-X

1 2 3 4 5 6 7 8 9 LB 11 10 09 08 07 06

Printed in the United States of America.

The Spirit *Within*

VOICES *of* YOUNG AUTHORS

Volume 2

Dear Readers,

On behalf of Alpha Kappa Alpha Sorority, Incorporated (AKA), I am delighted to present to you the second edition of *The Sprit Within: Voices of Young Authors*.
In 2008, Alpha Kappa Alpha Sorority will celebrate 100 years of service. Our membership of over 170,000 women has consciously chosen this affiliation as a means of self-fulfillment through volunteer service. Our motto of "service to all mankind" is reflected in the work we do and in the theme for this administration: "The SPIRIT of Alpha Kappa Alpha."

One of the targets of the 2002–2006 administration was to focus on young people and literacy. Specifically, an educational program initiative for children in second through sixth grades was implemented through the Young Authors Program, in partnership with the Metropolitan Teaching and Learning Company and Reggie Powe, its founder and president, to promote literacy by having children write and illustrate stories, as a means of becoming published authors. By the end of this administration, Alpha Kappa Alpha will have published two anthologies, celebrating 41 Young Authors and 41 honorable mention students from throughout the world! These were memorable times for the students, their parents, and AKA members in celebrating the Young Authors' strokes of imagination for, as Ralph Waldo Emerson said, "There are no days in life so memorable as those which vibrated to some stroke of the imagination."

With profound appreciation to Metro and Creative Curriculum Initiatives, our chapter members, and regional and national judges, I extend a heartfelt "thank you" for encouraging more than 44,000 children from around the world to participate in our Young Authors program.

Congratulations and best wishes to the Young Authors and their families! We look forward to your continued literary success as a future Maya Angelou or James Baldwin.

Sincerely,

Linda Marie White

Linda Marie White
26th National President
Alpha Kappa Alpha Sorority, Incorporated

Board of Directors
Alpha Kappa Alpha Sorority, Incorporated

Linda M. White
National President
Chicago, Illinois

Barbara A. McKinzie
National First Vice President
Chicago, Illinois

Nekeidra C. Brown
National Second Vice President
Houston, Texas

Carolyn House Stewart, Esquire
National Secretary
Tampa, Florida

Berna D. Greer
National Treasurer
Houston, Texas

Rachel Ashburn Mallory
National Parliamentarian
Columbus, Ohio

Candice Calhoun
National Undergraduate Member-at-Large
Oxford, Ohio

Erica S. Horton
National Undergraduate Member-at-Large
Milwaukee, Wisconsin

Joy Elaine Daley
North Atlantic Regional Director
Bronx, New York

Caroline L. Lattimore, Ph.D.
Mid-Atlantic Regional Director
Chapel Hill, North Carolina

Irene W. McCollom
South Atlantic Regional Director
Orangeburg, South Carolina

Pamela L. Redden, M.D.
Great Lakes Regional Director
Cleveland, Ohio

Cynthia J. Finch
South Eastern Regional Director
Knoxville, Tennessee

Tari T. Bradford
South Central Regional Director
Haughton, Louisiana

Dorothy W. Buckhanan
Central Regional Director
Milwaukee, Wisconsin

Betty Davis-Gause
Mid-Western Regional Director
Des Moines, Iowa

E. LaVonne Lewis
Far Western Regional Director
Las Vegas, Nevada

Nadine C. Bonds
International Regional Director
Indianapolis, Indiana

Betty N. James, Ed.D
Executive Director
Alpha Kappa Alpha Sorority, Incorporated
Chicago, Illinois

Dear Friends,

"Whatever you can do or dream you can, begin it. Boldness has genius, power, and magic in it," according to Johann Wolfgang von Goethe. Dreaming, boldness, power, and magic were some of the key elements Alpha Kappa Alpha Sorority, Incorporated utilized to improve the reading and writing skills of young children in grades 2–6 from around the world, through the implementation of the Young Authors Program.

On behalf of the National Program Committee of Alpha Kappa Alpha Sorority, I congratulate and thank the more than 44,000 young people who participated in our Young Authors Program. Over 323 Alpha Kappa Alpha chapters' winning entries were submitted from their local communities. Each chapter submitted her winning entries to our regional judges, and the regional Young Author winners were in competition to become our national winners.

The 21 Young Author national winners who are published in this anthology are presenting some exceptional stories and poems for you to read. Some will make you laugh. Some will make you cry. But they all will make you feel wonderful, because of the creative writing talents and skills these children possess. We proudly feature a student from the Mississippi School for the Blind (MSB) in this edition. We extend appreciation to Dr. Rosie Pridgen and the MSB for translating our first Young Authors anthology into Braille.

Indeed, we are grateful to Metropolitan Teaching and Learning Company, Creative Curriculum Initiatives (CCI), Reggie Powe, Jason Powe, Judy Rosenbaum, and the many other staff members of CCI who worked with us in publishing this anthology. Appreciation is further extended to the local, regional, and national judges and all members of Alpha Kappa Alpha Sorority. The parents of these Young Authors are also to be commended for the support they have given to these young people in their quest for knowledge as creative leaders of tomorrow.

Winston Churchill once said, "The empires of the future are the empires of the mind." Our greatest hope is that the children's "spirit within" will more fluidly connect to the "empires of their minds," as they journey to become empire builders.

Enjoy!

Juanita S. Doty

Juanita Sims Doty, Ed.D.
Chairman
National Program Committee
Alpha Kappa Alpha Sorority, Incorporated

National Program Committee
Alpha Kappa Alpha Sorority, Incorporated

Juanita Sims Doty, Ed.D.
Chairman

Nekeidra C. Brown
National Second Vice President

Rose Butler-Hayes, Ed.D.
Central Region

Jan M. Carpenter-Baker
Mid-Western Region

Sharon Brown Harriott
South Atlantic Region

Kimberly McLurkin-Harris
North Atlantic Region

Charlene Truitt Nelson
Great Lakes Region

Irene T. Outlaw, Ph.D.
Far Western Region

Ellenor C. Paul
International Region

Faye Pond-Haygood
South Eastern Region

Shuana Sims, Ph.D.
Mid-Atlantic Region

Cheryl Hegwood Williams
South Central Region

Contents

2 Letter from Linda White, President
3 Board of Directors
4 Letter from Juanita Sims Doty, Chairman, National Program Committee
5 National Program Committee

Young Authors, Grades 2–3

12 The Day I Went Around the World
by Sh'Zavia Hill
South Eastern

14 Friendship
by Stécie Guibert
Mid-Atlantic

18 Sally and the Giant
by ZaKiria Mays
South Atlantic

24 The Squirrel Attack
by Peyton Hawkins
North Atlantic

28 Two Girls in a Different World
    by Azuré Smith
    South Central

34 Just Me and My Grammy
    by Chanel Smith
    Far Western

38 The Person I Admire Most
    by Kristen Pratt
    International

42 The Skunk's Stink Gland
    by Yvan Quinn
    Mid-Western

46 Friendship
    by MyKayla Strother
    Great Lakes

50 Golden Sunshine
    by Lisa Wilson
    Central

Young Authors, Grades 4–6

56   An African American Dream Mom
       by Rakia Levesque
       Great Lakes

62   I Love Life, and I Want to Live
       by Ashley Buckner
       North Atlantic

68   Thankful for What I Got
       by Starre Williams
       Central

76   Mantack, The Wandering Wolf
       by Rowan Thompson
       Mid-Western

84   Pieces of the Puzzle
       by Tommie Sierra Middleton
       South Atlantic

88   My Dad: The Person I Admire Most
       by Rhen Bass II
       Far Western

94   The Clydesdale's Courage
        by Alexandra Bender
        Mid-Atlantic

98   Me, Myself, and I
        by Kelsey Gray
        South Eastern

106   My Most Unforgettable Experience
        by Tabitha Ritchie
        International

112   Yorktown's Lady Rattlesnakes
        by Andrea Lloyd
        Mississippi School for the Blind

118   Spring Makes Me Feel . . .
        by Jordan Wynn
        South Central

122   Young Author Biographies
133   Honorable Mention
136   National Judges
137   Regional Judges
140   Corporate Partners
141   Alpha Kappa Alpha Sorority,
        Incorporated: Who We Are
142   Index of Authors

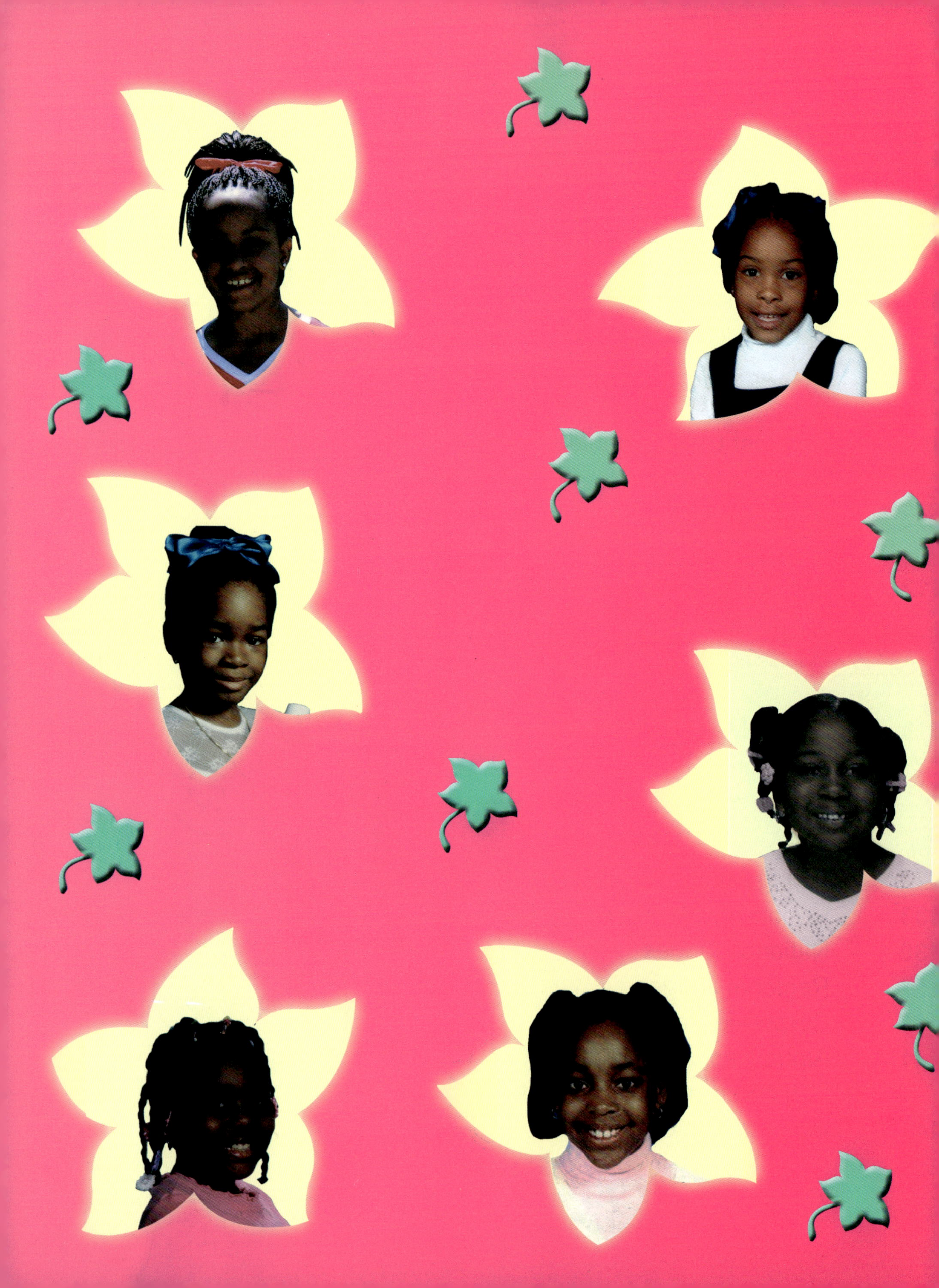

Young Authors
Grades 2–3

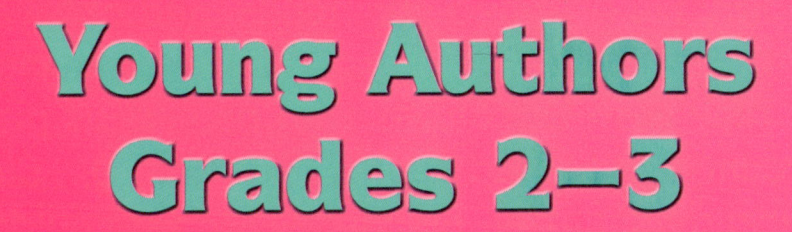

The Day I Went AROUND the World

by Sh'Zavia Hill
Illustrated by Otis Hughley

I had an amazing dream. My brother and I were sitting on the floor watching TV when we heard a knock. The door suddenly opened, and in came Dr. Clown. He grabbed our hands, and off we went in his three-seater airplane! We were having a great time with Dr. Clown, who bought us pizza, ice cream, candy, and apples. By then, Dr. Clown had already spent all his money, so we couldn't get any more apples. Instead, he gave me more pizza and ice cream, and then I had a nap. My brother was eating some pizza and ice cream, too.

It was almost suppertime, and we were still with Dr, Clown. When I looked down, I finally knew that we were going around the world. Then I shouted to my brother, "We're going around the world!"

As soon as my brother heard me, he tried to get away. I pulled him back and tightened his seat belt. My brother squirmed and wiggled. He really could wiggle! He was getting on my nerves.

Dr. Clown was still flying the three-seater airplane, and I had never seen a plane like that before. When he did the loops, I felt like I was going to fall. My head was starting to hurt, and my stomach was growling. I turned to Dr. Clown, but he had just fallen asleep. I hurried and grabbed the wheel. My head was really going to fall off if I didn't land soon.

In my dream, my bedtime had passed, and I was sleepy. My brother was already asleep. The plane landed by itself. Right then I woke up. And I never dreamed about Dr. Clown again!

Friendship

by Stécie Guibert

What does friendship mean to you? Friendship means many things to me. It means sharing, helping feeble people, giving, hugging, and just having fun together. You can be friends with anyone. It doesn't matter what you look like or where you're from. Friendship is special, and you need to share it with other people.

Come to Mount Eagle School, and see my friend Karla. We have a friendship to be admired. She comes from El Salvador, and I am from Haiti. We always play together and write notes to each other. Karla and I are together so much that we do our homework together. My mom lets me go to Karla's house. Sometimes her dad lets her come to my house. There are times that Karla and I get upset with each other, but we can still be friends. Whenever we have a problem, we just talk it out. Then we are back to being friends again. She never bosses me around. We will be friends forever and ever. I'm lucky to have a friend like her.

Another good friend of mine is named Sara. We always remember each other's birthday. She gives me stuff for my birthday. I give her stuff for her birthday. We also have so many things in common. Both of us are respectful and kind. Both of us are from countries other than the United States. I feel delighted about our friendship.

From the friendships I have with Sara and Karla, I have learned that we have to respect one another and show kindness. I have learned from Dr. Martin Luther King, Jr., too, and I am grateful to him. Dr. King fought for equality. Because of his bravery, now Karla, Sara, and I can be friends.

I have learned that it does not matter if we are from different countries, speak different languages, or look different. We still can be best friends. Friendship is like gold. You should value it and keep it close to your heart.

Sally
and the
Giant

by ZaKiria Mays

Once there was a girl named Sally who lived on a farm in Mississippi. Although Sally's father owned a farm, he didn't have a lot of animals. One day, Sally's mother said she would have to sell the family's talking pet cow if they ran out of food. Sally was very sad because she really loved their pet cow. Because she loved him so much, Sally tried to spend all the time she could with him until she had to sell him. They did a lot together. They played board games, video games, soccer, basketball, baseball, tennis, and other games.

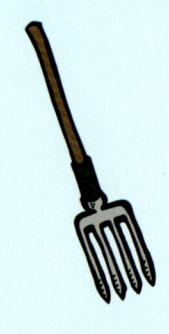

One day, while Sally was going for a walk with her pet cow, she met a giant named George.

"Hello!" said Sally.
"What are you doing on my property?" asked the giant.
"Nothing," replied Sally. "I was just taking my pet cow for a walk."
"You have a pet cow?" asked the giant.
"Yes!" Sally said.
"Do you have a problem with that?" the cow asked the giant.
"Yes," replied the giant. "You're on my property."
"Where do you live?" asked the cow.
"Right there in that big palace," said the giant, pointing to it.
"May we go into your palace?" asked the cow.
"Well, I guess so," the giant said.

When they walked into the palace, they didn't see anything but gold, gold, gold, and more gold! Sally was amazed. She had never seen so much gold in her whole life.

"Wow!" said Sally.

"You sure do have a big house," said the cow.

"And a lot of gold!" added Sally.

"May we have some?" asked the cow.

"What?" yelled George the Giant, with a mean look on his face. "I thought I just heard you ask for some of my gold."

"Why, yes, I did," replied the cow in a quiet voice.

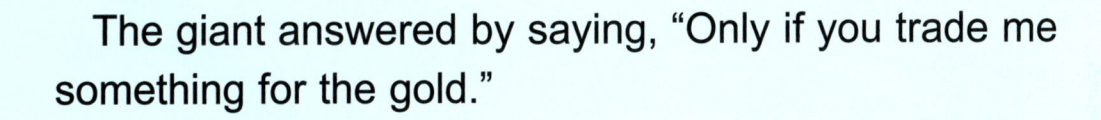

The giant answered by saying, "Only if you trade me something for the gold."

"Okay," said Sally. "We'll be right back!"

Sally and the cow went home to tell Sally's mom about the deal with George the Giant.

"I love it," said Sally's mom, "but what are we going to trade for the gold?"

"I don't know," said Sally, "but we'll have to find something."

Sally looked all over her house, but she couldn't find anything to trade. She kept looking until she finally found the perfect thing, a pink pearl necklace that her grandmother had given her years ago. Although the pearl necklace was special and meant a lot to Sally, she was willing to part with it. She did not want to lose the family's pet cow! Sally kissed the pearl necklace, wrapped it gently in tissue, and took it back to the giant's palace. The cow was touched by her kindness, for he knew that Sally really liked her pearl necklace a lot.

When Sally saw George, she lowered her head, handed him the tissue package, and said, "Here you go!"

George opened the tissue, took out the pearl necklace, held it up, and smiled like a big happy dog.

"And here you go," said George the Giant, as he handed some gold to Sally.

When Sally got home, she showed her mom the gold that George the Giant had given her for the necklace. Sally's family used the gold to buy food, and, of course, they didn't have to sell their pet cow after all.

Many people think that friends must be human. Sally doesn't agree with this belief at all. Sally's friend was the family's talking pet cow, and she loved her pet cow just as much as she loved her human friends. This story just proves that friends can come in all shapes, colors, and sizes.

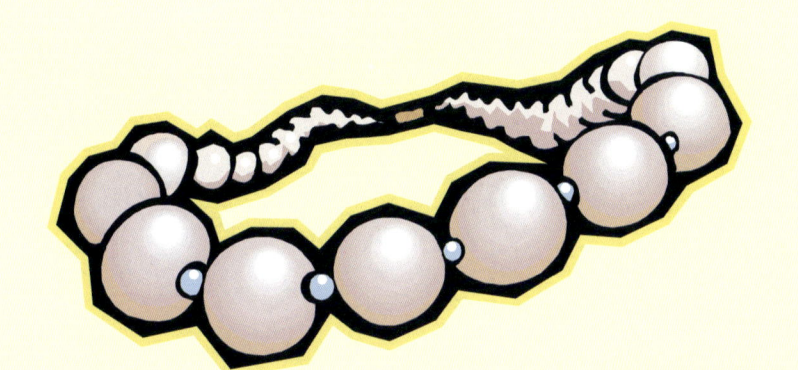

23

The Squirrel Attack

by Peyton Hawkins

Last winter was so cold that it felt like the inside of a refrigerator. Icicles hung from the roof like ice-cream cones. I looked out of the upstairs window at the long, skinny, pointed crystals. Suddenly, I could hear strange shushing noises above me. I shivered, but it wasn't from the cold!

I didn't think any more about the sounds. Instead, I went shopping and ran errands with Mom. It started to snow while we were out, so we hurried home. I looked up at the roof, now completely covered with snow, and I couldn't believe what I saw! There were a dozen paw prints leading to one corner of the rooftop. And it definitely wasn't Rudolph and his reindeer friends!

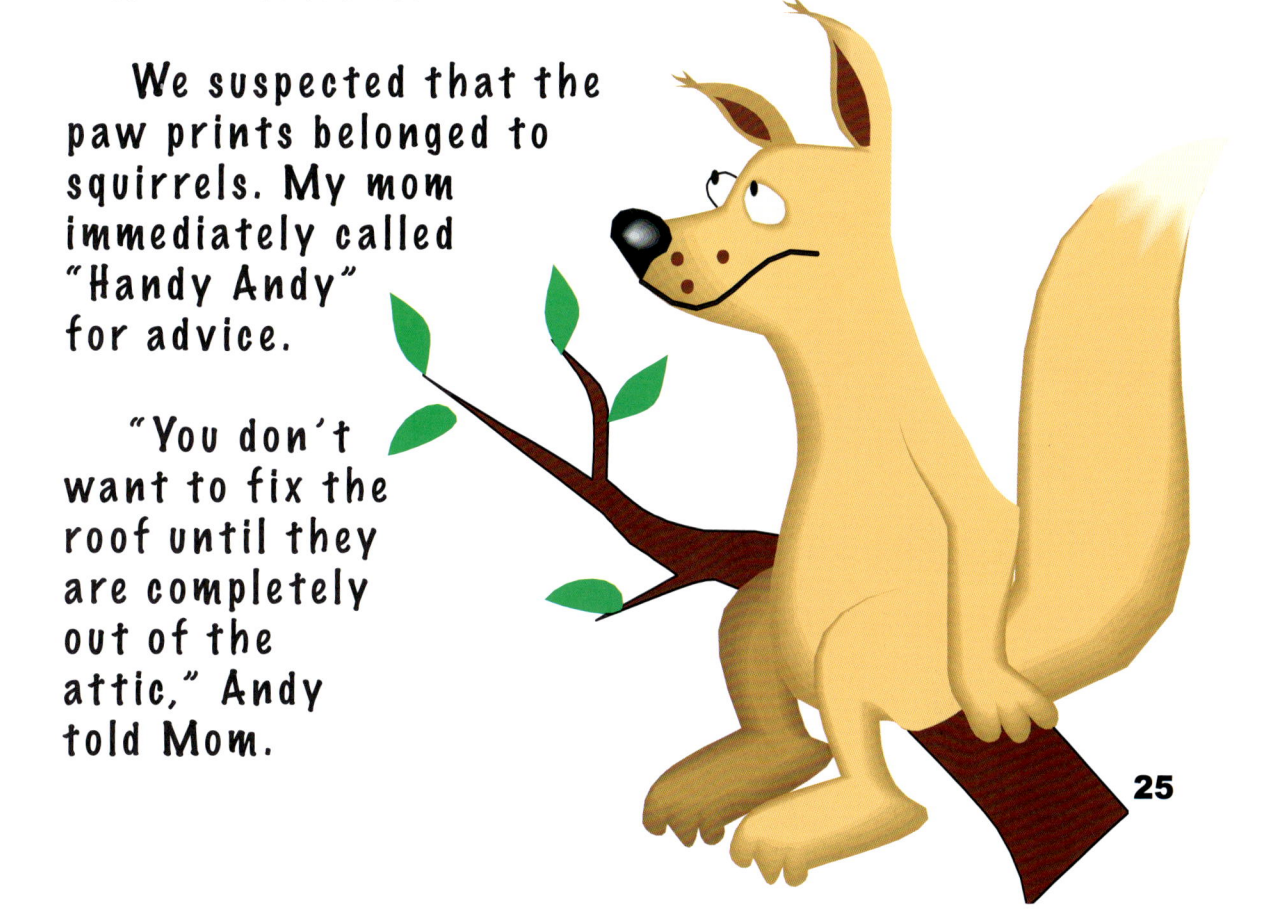

We suspected that the paw prints belonged to squirrels. My mom immediately called "Handy Andy" for advice.

"You don't want to fix the roof until they are completely out of the attic," Andy told Mom.

We called the pest control company, and they set out three large cages. The serviceman smeared peanut butter on slices of apple, and in no time he had caught six squirrels! Was our attic their Holiday Inn?

My dad drove the squirrels ten miles away to Cooper River Park and released them. We were certain that they would not be back. We believed that all was well since we didn't hear any noises. We each gave a big sigh of relief. They had driven us nuts for long enough!

After one week with no nut-collecting friends, Mom called "Handy Andy" to come out and fix the tiny hole in the roof. Amazingly, the hole was only the size of a quarter!

That night I had a dream of a squirrel house party. There was a DJ scratching the records, and all the squirrels —"Yo-yo-yo,"— were dancing!

The next day Mom and I were out running errands again. Mom's cell phone rang while we were in the car. I could tell that it was Dad's voice, and he sounded excited.

Mom gave me the phone. "You won't believe this!" Dad announced. "I found a mother and two baby squirrels in the closet." The squirrels had eaten a huge hole through the Sheetrock and let themselves in.

Mom considered not even going home after this. She kept saying, "...in the *closet*, ...in the *closet*..."

I knew that she was feeling quite jittery. "Don't worry, I'll protect you, Mom," I told her.

But it was Dad who bravely caught the squirrels. He put the mother and her babies into a cage and took them all to Cooper River Park. When he returned, he chopped down branches from the big tree closest to the house. I guess he didn't want more little critters visiting our house.

Even though he needed to sit down for about fifteen minutes afterward, Dad was our hero!

TWO GIRLS IN A DIFFERENT WORLD

Written and illustrated by Azuré Smith

Tomorrow was the first day of school, and Trina was very excited. She was going to start the fourth grade at a new school called Smith Elementary. Trina could not wait to go to school and make new friends.

On the first day of school, Trina met Nancy. Nancy was very pretty and had the prettiest dress Trina had ever seen. Nancy's parents owned a huge shopping mall and were very rich. Nancy got everything she wanted and bragged to all the girls about all the toys, clothes, and money she had.

Even though Nancy's bragging was annoying, Trina wished she could switch places with Nancy and have everything that Nancy had. Trina's parents were farm workers from the country, and they were poor. For the rest of the day, Nancy continued to brag about her life. This made Trina very sad.

Later that night after Trina brushed her teeth and got ready for bed, she looked out of her bedroom window. She imagined all the things that she would get if she was rich.

Suddenly she noticed a shooting star in the sky. "I wish I could switch places with Nancy," she said. Then Trina closed her eyes and went to bed.

The next morning, Trina woke up and thought about what she would wear to school that day. She didn't have many fancy clothes like Nancy. But when she opened her eyes, she was not in her bedroom!

Trina didn't know where she was. She stepped down from the pink princess bed and walked to the closet. It was filled with lots of beautiful clothes.

Suddenly Trina heard a woman's voice call, "Nancy! Nancy! Nancy, come down and get your breakfast." Trina looked in the mirror and screamed. She was in Nancy's body!

At Trina's house that morning, Nancy was going through the same thing. Not knowing what to do, both girls tried to act the way each thought the other would act. At least until they got to school!

At school, Trina waited for Nancy, and they talked about what happened. They agreed to try to act like each other until they could figure out how to switch back. Nancy was upset because she did not want to be poor. She liked to brag about everything that she had.

All day long, Trina had to brag as if she were Nancy. When school was over, she went home to Nancy's house. There, she had to listen to more bragging from Nancy's family. Trina even had to deal with Nancy's annoying little brother. She thought back to the beginning of the day. When she had first wakened, it was nice to see her beautiful clothes and room. But now she missed her own family. Her family never bragged about things. And though they worried about money, they usually talked about a lot of other stuff that was much more interesting.

During her day at school, Nancy had to be kind all day and not talk about money or toys. When school was over, Nancy went home to Trina's house. She had to find other things to talk about with Trina's family. They laughed and joked with one another. When one of the other kids told about catching a ball or getting an answer right at school, everyone else praised that kid.

The girls lived in each other's bodies for one week. Trina was upset because she would rather have her family's love and kindness than money and pretty clothes. During that same time, Nancy was surprised to find that she was enjoying living with people who didn't seem to have a lot of money or fancy things. They were so kind and loving to her.

One week later, when the girls woke up, they were both back in their own bodies, sleeping in their own beds. They were so happy! At school, they talked with each other about what they had learned. Both agreed that love and kindness matter much more than money.

Nancy promised that she would never brag again, and Trina promised that she would be grateful for all that she had. Even though they had been very different at first, Trina and Nancy became the best of friends.

Just Me and My Grammy

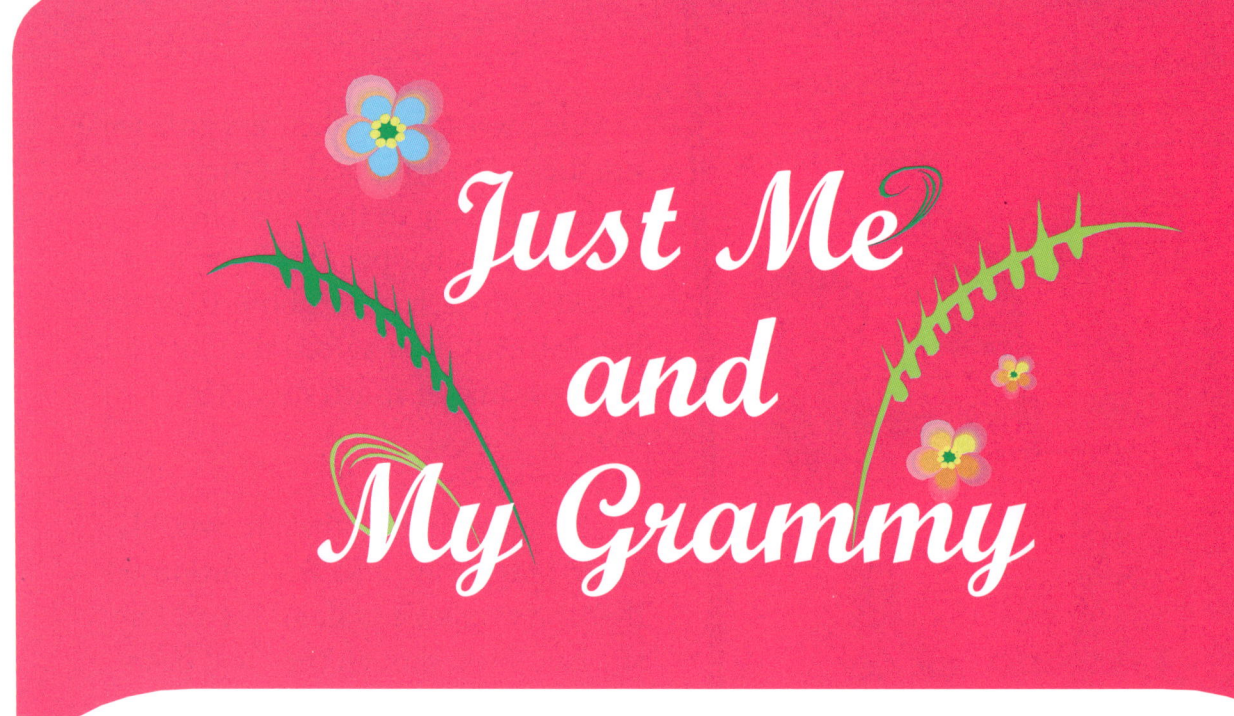

by Chanel Smith

"Chanel, I remember when you were in your mama's tummy!" "Little girl, stop growing!" "I knew you would be something great!" "I'm sooo proud of you!" "That's my baby!" These are just some of the things my grandmother says to me almost every time she sees me. I get excited when I go to Grammy's because I know we are going to cook and go to Costco, "our" Ralph's, or the the nail shop. Why do I admire and love her so much? I love the special time we spend together . . . just my Grammy and me.

We get in her shiny black car and ride down Seventh Avenue. Just about everyone knows her and waves as we go by. We speak to her special friend, the old lady on the corner. Her husband died, just like my Grammy's husband, Poppie. Now it is just the lady by herself, just like my Grammy.

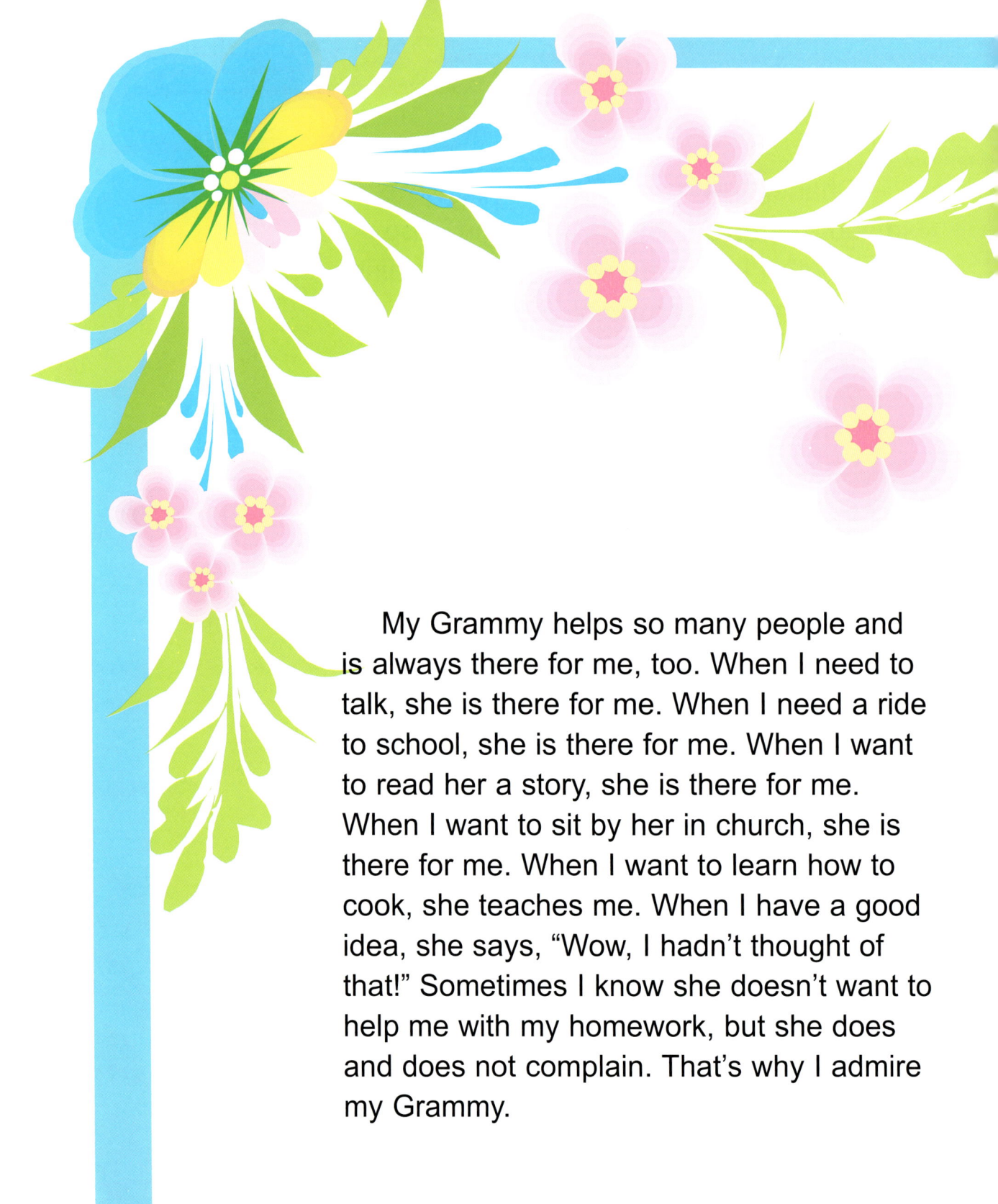

My Grammy helps so many people and is always there for me, too. When I need to talk, she is there for me. When I need a ride to school, she is there for me. When I want to read her a story, she is there for me. When I want to sit by her in church, she is there for me. When I want to learn how to cook, she teaches me. When I have a good idea, she says, "Wow, I hadn't thought of that!" Sometimes I know she doesn't want to help me with my homework, but she does and does not complain. That's why I admire my Grammy.

I enjoy the time we spend together on the weekends. Sometimes, we climb in our favorite green fluffy chair and pull back the wood handle to relax our legs. My Grammy always complains that now I am getting too big to sit in the same chair with her. I just laugh and snuggle up to her. We tuck our favorite soft green blanket over our legs and stick the top of the blanket under our chins. Sometimes we watch our favorite TV shows, and other times we read. Sometimes we just sit and listen to music. When we hear a good old school song, we jump up and start to dance. After it is over, we jump back into our chair. And when it's time to go to bed, I give her a goodnight kiss and say, "Grammy, I love you." Then I thank God for my Grammy.

THE PERSON I ADMIRE MOST

by Kristen Pratt

The person I admire most is my teacher. Her name is Miss Paul. She is five feet tall, has dark brown skin and black hair, and wears glasses.

    She is a very hardworking teacher. She teaches us many subjects like mathematics, language, and comprehension. She has a lot of papers to grade and a lot of books to mark. She only gets one break and lunch, which is one hour, and then she goes back to work. Sometimes she hardly leaves the classroom because she is so busy. Miss Paul teaches us songs, too. She taught us "If I Were a Butterfly" and the second part of

"He's Still Working on Me." Miss Paul is a very intelligent person because she knows almost everything. She is able to answer most of our questions. If she cannot, she will tell us to look it up in the dictionary or search the Internet.

My teacher is thoughtful. She is determined to get our grades up. She does not ignore us as we are doing our work. Sometimes she walks around the room and checks our work. She always makes sure we understand what was taught. If we do not understand, she thinks of a way for us to understand it.

Miss Paul is encouraging. She gives us stamps, clasps, and stickers. Miss Paul makes sure that we keep a journal and that we read books to get writing ideas. She also lets us use the centers around the classroom when we have finished our work.

My teacher is very friendly. She lets me and the other students help her in class. After school, she lets us clean up and keep her company. Sometimes she helps the other teachers with their work. She also takes time to talk with our parents. She is hardworking, intelligent, encouraging, and thoughtful. Miss Paul is a person I can look up to. She is very thoughtful as a teacher because she is teaching us how to become good citizens.

The Skunk's Stink Gland

by Yvan Quinn

One morning I woke up with a skunk's stink gland. I didn't notice because I had a stuffy nose and when I got dressed, everything seemed normal. But when I went to the kitchen . . .

. . . my mom fainted because of the smell!!! My dad and I carried her to her room. She stayed there for a little bit.

My dad went to the doctor with my mom and me. The doctor said that he couldn't find anything wrong. Then the stink gland acted up, and my mom fainted again!!! The doctor told me to move along. Then he yelled, "YUCK!!!!!"

43

It was time to go to school. When I got there, the stink came back. The teacher fainted. When she came to, she made me go to the nurse. At first, the nurse found nothing wrong. But then she yelled, "YUCK!!!!!" And she fainted, too.

Then I had an idea. I went to the principal's office. At first, he told me to go back to my classroom. But then he yelled, "YUCK!!!" and he got out of there.

I started to make changes with the principal's stuff. I changed the schedule for the day. The entire day was either recess or games. The rest of the day was really fun for everyone, especially for me. I won every game of Twister. I never got tagged in tag, so I was never It.

The entire day was fun, except for trying to sleep at night. I didn't have a stuffy nose anymore, so I couldn't sleep!!! I yelled, "YUCK!!!!!!" Finally, at midnight, I fell asleep. The next morning, I woke up. I smelled around me. The skunk's stink gland was…gone! So I was pretty sure I was normal. I did cross eyes to make sure I was normal. It felt easier than usual. But when I went to the kitchen…my mom fainted!!! I asked how I was different since the skunk's stink gland was gone. My dad said that I had iguana eyes. I said, "OH, GREAT!!!"

Friendship

by MyKayla Strother

Friendship is important because you will need someone to play with, and a friend can be your playmate. Also, you can call your friend and talk on the phone when you are lonely or visit at your friend's house on the weekends.

If you get into a fight with your friend, you can make up and forgive the friend because friends are important and everyone should have a friend. **Friendship** is important if you are an only child because it can help you when you are feeling lonely.

You can also have friendships with your brothers and sisters. I have a brother and sister, and they are my friends. Even though sometimes they annoy me, I still treat them as my friends. They are my friends because they play with me and we talk about things that are important to us. I am very glad to have a brother and sister who care about me and love me.

Friends who aren't related should also care about each other and love each other like brothers or sisters.

Friends don't always have to be people. A pet can be a friend, too. If you get a pet as a friend, you will have a lot of work to do to care for it, but you won't mind because friends help each other, even if the friend is an animal.

I wrote a poem about what it takes to be a good friend and to have a good friendship. I hope you enjoy it. It is called "What Friendship Means to Me."

F is for friendship
R is for respect
I is for independence
E is for excellence
N is for niceness
D is for devotion
S is for self-confidence
H is for honesty
I is for intelligence
P is for peacefulness

These are all the things I feel are important to being a friend and having friends.

Golden Sunshine

by Lisa Wilson

One dark and cloudy morning at 9:15 A.M., a street cleaner stopped me and Mom and asked if we wanted to hear a story. "Sure, why not," I replied.

He began his story . . .

Back in the year 1980 in Atlanta, Georgia, there used to live a man named Damon Walker. Damon was a widower, but then he got married again to a woman who was as pretty as a rose. Some people called her Golden because she was so light-skinned. At this time, Golden was beautiful, 20 years old, and pregnant with her first baby. Golden was very happy about being pregnant.

Her next-door neighbor would ask her, "You sure you having a baby? It's gotta be time for you to have that baby."

"Stop joking around," Golden would say. "I can't wait till she gets here. I'm naming her Sunshine."

"It's a girl?" asked the neighbor.

"Shh!" Golden whispered. She didn't want anyone to know that the baby was a girl until after the birth.

One day it was storming badly. The raindrops were so large it looked as though it was raining gumdrops. The lightning was so bright it looked like fireworks. Soon Golden was bored with watching the rain in the window across from her bed.

The power had been out in the house most of the morning and had just come back on. Golden thought about popping some popcorn, but she decided she wasn't hungry. So she went to the video store and rented a movie. When she got back home, she watched the movie. Around 1:00 P.M., Golden heard a car door slam. It was Damon.

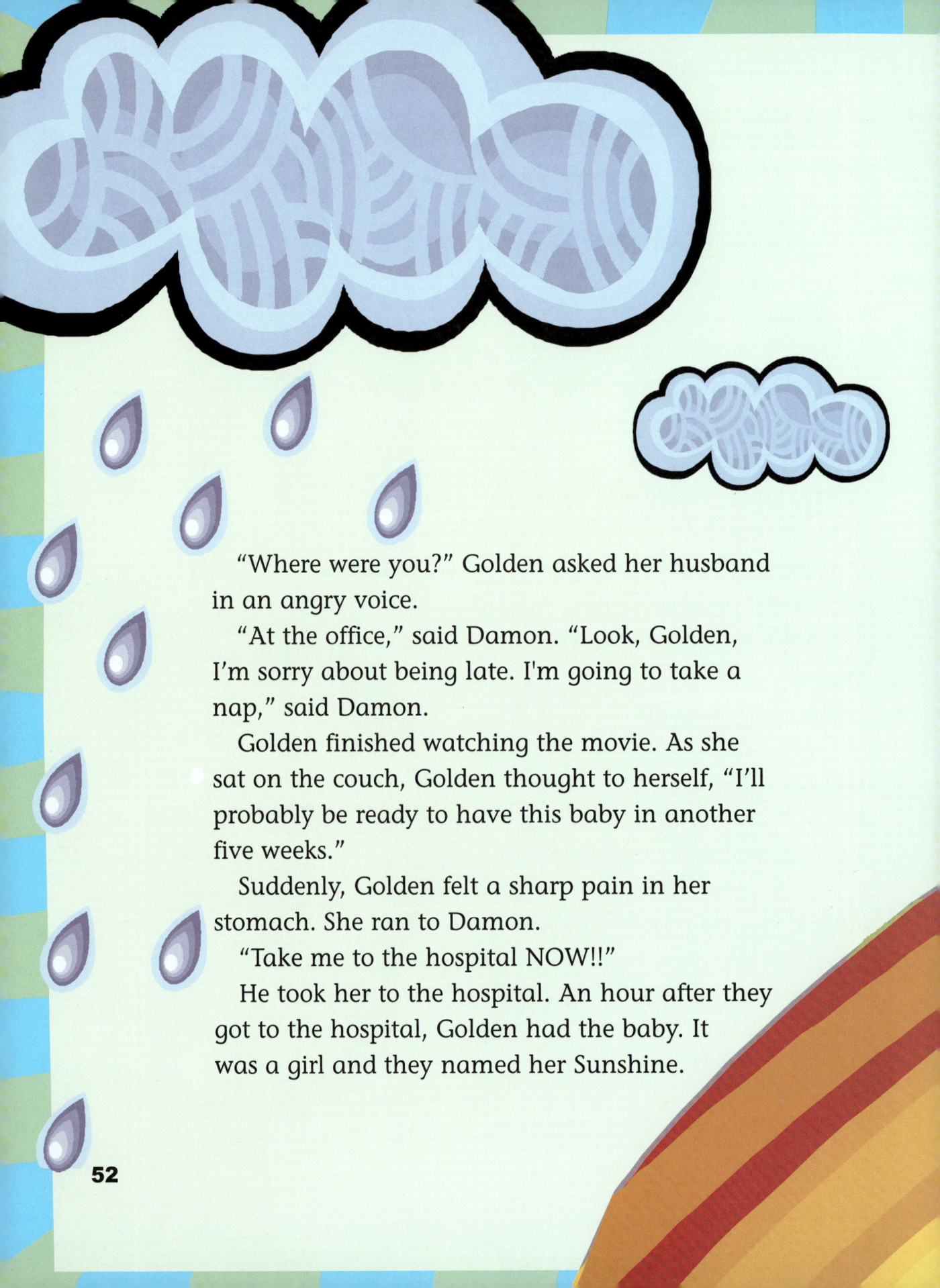

"Where were you?" Golden asked her husband in an angry voice.

"At the office," said Damon. "Look, Golden, I'm sorry about being late. I'm going to take a nap," said Damon.

Golden finished watching the movie. As she sat on the couch, Golden thought to herself, "I'll probably be ready to have this baby in another five weeks."

Suddenly, Golden felt a sharp pain in her stomach. She ran to Damon.

"Take me to the hospital NOW!!"

He took her to the hospital. An hour after they got to the hospital, Golden had the baby. It was a girl and they named her Sunshine.

"Why are you telling us this story?" I asked the street cleaner.

"You remind me of Sunshine," he said.

"How do I remind you of her?"

"As you walked down the street with your mother, you seemed so happy, just the way she was," he said. "My daughter, Sunshine, grew to be a sweet, cute, happy little girl. At the age of 8, we found out Sunshine had leukemia. Sunshine came into our lives on May 9, 1980, and she left us 16 years ago today, July 12, 1990."

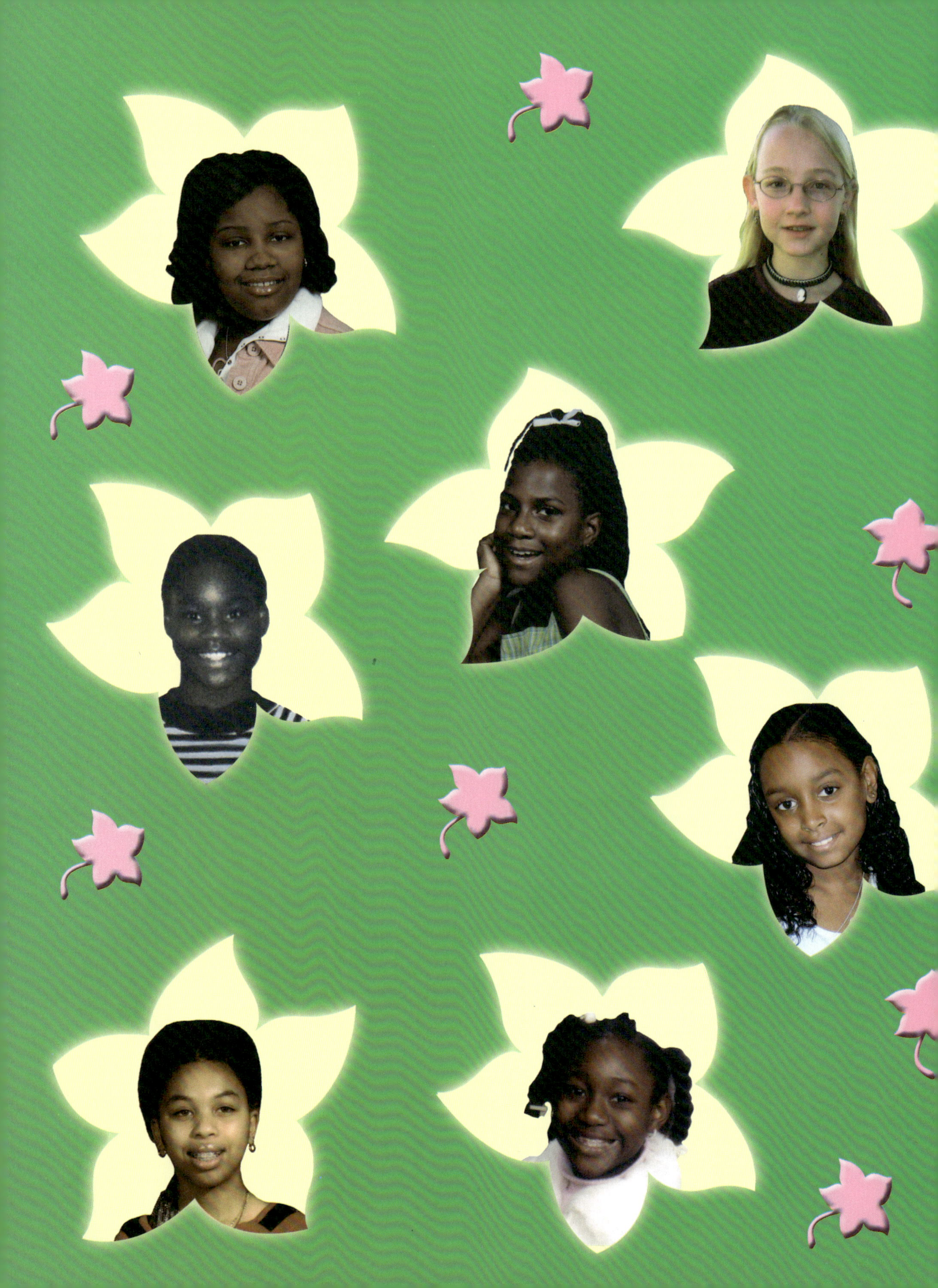

Young Authors
Grades 4–6

An African American Dream Mom

by Rakia Levesque

As you read this story, you will begin to understand what I mean by "an African American Dream Mom." You will learn why I admire my mom as an African American Dream Mom. So sit back, relax, and get ready for a fulfilling journey.

When you hear the words Dream Mom, you probably think of a mom who is famous, beautiful, and intelligent. However, that is not my idea of a Dream Mom. My idea is one who would struggle through thick and thin, or even lie down and die for her children.

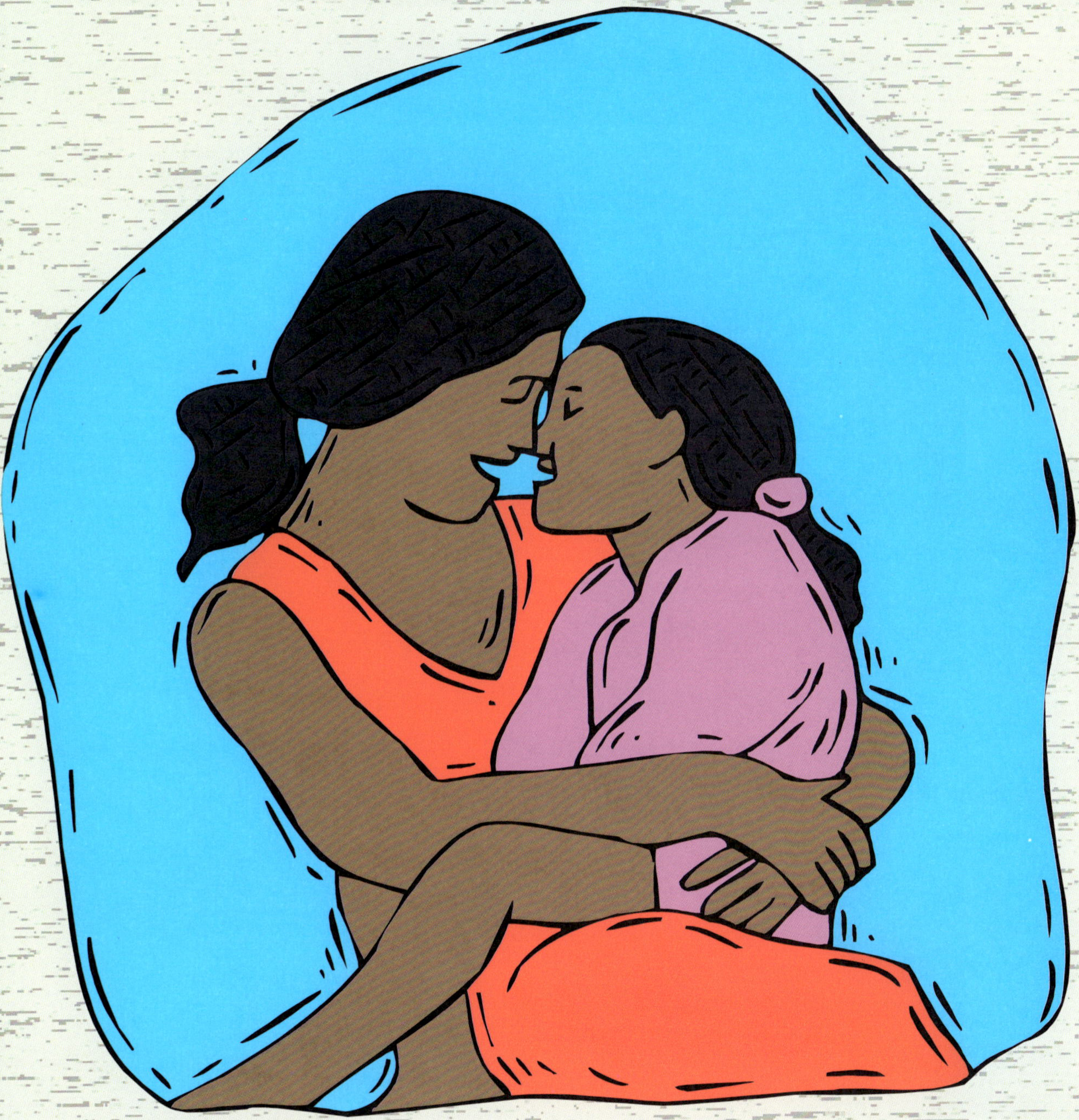

My mom was a single parent as she raised me. We struggled every now and then, but she never gave up. She always kept her faith. On the days when we had little to eat, my mom would give her food to me and say, "You are a bundle of joy sent from Heaven. You will always be my top priority, no matter what we go through in life." She always told me that she was both my mother and my father because she did the job of both since my dad was not around. To this very day, my mom plays both roles, which is a very tough job.

As my mom and I struggled day after day, I often thought about why my mother had to face such a hard task. Through the years, as I grew older, I saw that the toughness of her task was what made her into an independent, strong, successful, out-of-the-ordinary, special African American mom. Throughout the days, my mom faced many trials and tribulations, but every time she did, she kept going. She never gave up. After a while, she got a job, a car, and a house.

When my mom got a job, she had to work overtime a lot. She saved up all her overtime money to buy a car. When Mom got her car, she made getting me to school and to church every Sunday her top priorities. Mom wanted me to grow up valuing education and my community. I thank my mom for making sure that I grew up in the church, because if she hadn't, I wouldn't be the successful young African American girl that I am today.

Now that I am older, I understand the task of an African American Dream Mom in a much deeper way. Each new day, I try to take the same successful steps that my mom took. Now that I am older, I understand how someone becomes an African American Dream Mom.

A mother's tasks are to love her child dearly every day and to help a wandering child find his or her way.
A mother's tasks cannot be measured because they never end.
This is why we call Mom our most hardworking friend.
This is the reason why I admire my mom as an African American Dream Mom.

I Love Life, and I Want to Live

by Ashley Buckner

What is life?
That is the question to ask.
Life is something you do not play with.
Life is something powerful.
Life is something everyone craves.
No one wants to lose his or her life.
I love life, and I want to live.

Who started this violence?
We did!!
We as the human race started the violence.
That is why there are guns.
That is why someone dies each day.
But, I love life, and I want to live.

We are the ones deceiving
each other.
We are the ones who stand and look
at each other lie down and die
helplessly.
We as the human race need to put a stop
to the violence.
Why do we live when all we do is kill?
That, no one really knows.
I love life, and I want to live.

It is hard living in a dog-eat-dog violent world.
In my life I have seen verbal violence,
physical violence, and emotional violence.
I have seen it all.
I have seen much in my twelve years.
It is so unfair.
Somebody stop them!!
I want to live!!
Don't you?

Although I am only twelve, I have a lot to say.
Many people don't get to see the sunlight
　in the morning.
My life will not be cut short.
It will not end by violence.
My life will be long and filled with education.

There are many things in life that need to be explored,
such as growing up and college.
I will be very dedicated to living in a nonviolent world.
I want to live a life of peace.

I want to live my life my way.
I will not be a victim of violence.
I will go to college and get a degree.
Maybe I'll try to get two or three.
I want to accomplish things I never thought I could.

I love life because of my family.
I want to live for my family,
the Holy One, and me.
I want to grow up, get a job,
and have a family.
I want to live to see my family
make it in life, just as I will.
I want to live to see my children accomplish
more than I did.
I want to live to see my children have
children. I want to live!!

There are many questions that are waiting
to be answered.
I want to enjoy the wonders of life!
I want to live because there are many secrets
that need to be revealed.
When I grow up, I can share my knowledge
with the world.
I love life, and I want to live!!

Although I'm only a child, I have older friends asking me for advice.
So I solve their problems and my own.
I love life because I get to develop good relationships with people.

I love my life, and I want to live it.
I am not a materialistic person.
That's just me.
My life may not be perfect, but that is okay. I cherish it well.
I love life . . .
. . . . And I want to live.

THANKFUL FOR WHAT I GOT

A screenplay by Starre Williams

Scene 1
(Morning, inside the house where ANGIE and NICOLE, both foster children, live with their FOSTER MAMA.)

FOSTER MAMA
Who was that at the door, Angie?

ANGIE
I don't know.

FOSTER MAMA (angrily)
Don't you talk to me in that tone of voice. Go to your room right now till I tell you to come out.

ANGIE
I hate you—I wish I had never met you!

(ANGIE runs to her room. NICOLE follows her.)

ANGIE
The woman at the door was my real mom. I've been talking to her every day for a while.

NICOLE
(Very surprised)
What?

ANGIE
Yeah, she is pretty cool. You should meet her. I'm planning to run away and stay with her.

NICOLE
What? Why? When?

ANGIE
Come with me?

NICOLE
I don't know.

ANGIE
Foster Mama is upstairs putting Jasmine to sleep. We can easily sneak out right now.

NICOLE
(paces the room and thinks for a while)
I have known you since we were two. You're my best friend, not just my foster sister. If you left, my life would be miserable. I guess...I guess I'll come with you.

ANGIE
Great! Pack—let's go.

Scene 2

(The next day, inside the home of ANGIE'S birth mother, SUSAN. ANGIE and SUSAN are watching a horror movie. NICOLE just sits there looking uncomfortable.)

ANGIE

This is the life! My foster mama would never allow me to do this.

SUSAN

She is quite the square.

ANGIE

I know. I am so glad I met you.

NICOLE

Angie, I need to talk to you. Come outside.

(The two go outside.)

ANGIE

What's the problem?

NICOLE

I don't like this place at all. Let's go back home right now!

ANGIE

But this *is* home.

NICOLE

Not to me.

ANGIE

Why are you so difficult?

NICOLE

Me! Difficult. You have really lost your mind. I'm leaving right now.

(NICOLE acts as though she is headed for the bus stop.)

ANGIE

(grabbing her hand)
Please don't go! You're the only real friend I have.

NICOLE

All right. I'll stay.

Scene 3

(The same location, early evening. SUSAN comes in after she has been out most of the day.)

ANGIE

There's no food in the house. We're hungry.

SUSAN

So what you want me to do? I'm no cook. Go get your own food.

ANGIE

How? Where?

SUSAN

What do I care? I'm not the one who's hungry.

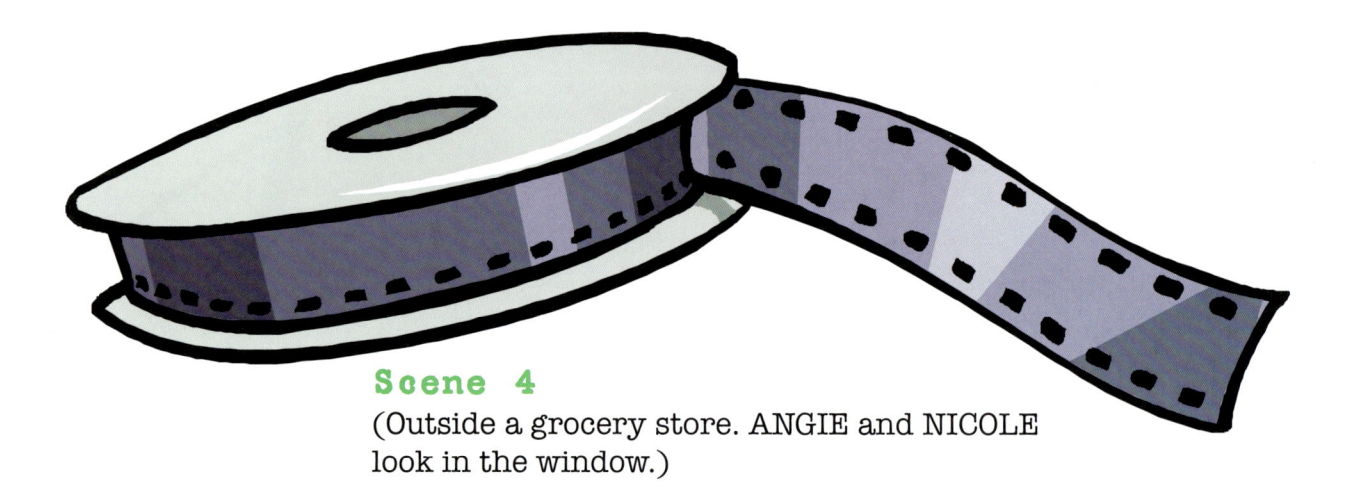

Scene 4
(Outside a grocery store. ANGIE and NICOLE look in the window.)

NICOLE
Look what's happened to us. We used to take eating for granted. Now we're looking in a store window at food we can't afford to buy. Do you still think this is quite the life?

ANGIE
(crying)
I am so sorry I got you in this mess. I thought my mom was really cool, but now I know she doesn't care about anyone but herself.

NICOLE
Don't cry—I'll be here for you till the end. Wait . . . do you hear that voice?

(ANGIE and NICOLE go closer to the store's entrance. Inside, they see FOSTER MAMA.)

FOSTER MAMA
Do you know where 1716 North Sylvan Street is?

STORE ATTENDANT
Sure, you take a left on St. Louis Avenue and walk about two blocks.

NICOLE
(hearing the voice)
That's our foster mama! What's she doing down here?

ANGIE
(stops crying and looks up)
You're right. There she is by the counter. Did she come looking for us? Mama! Mama!

(Both girls run into FOSTER MAMA's arms, wailing.)

FOSTER MAMA
(crying) Oh, my precious girls. I should spank you both, but I'm so glad you're safe. Oh, my girls.

BOTH GIRLS
We're sorry. We're sorry.

FOSTER MAMA
If you're down here, you're with Susan, right? I thought I saw her hanging around the house the other day.

NICOLE
Mama, you don't know what it was like at her house.

FOSTER MAMA
Yes I do. I've seen it.

ANGIE
How did you know my real mom?

FOSTER MAMA
'Cause Susan is my sister and I am your auntie.

ANGIE
(out of breath)
What? You! You!

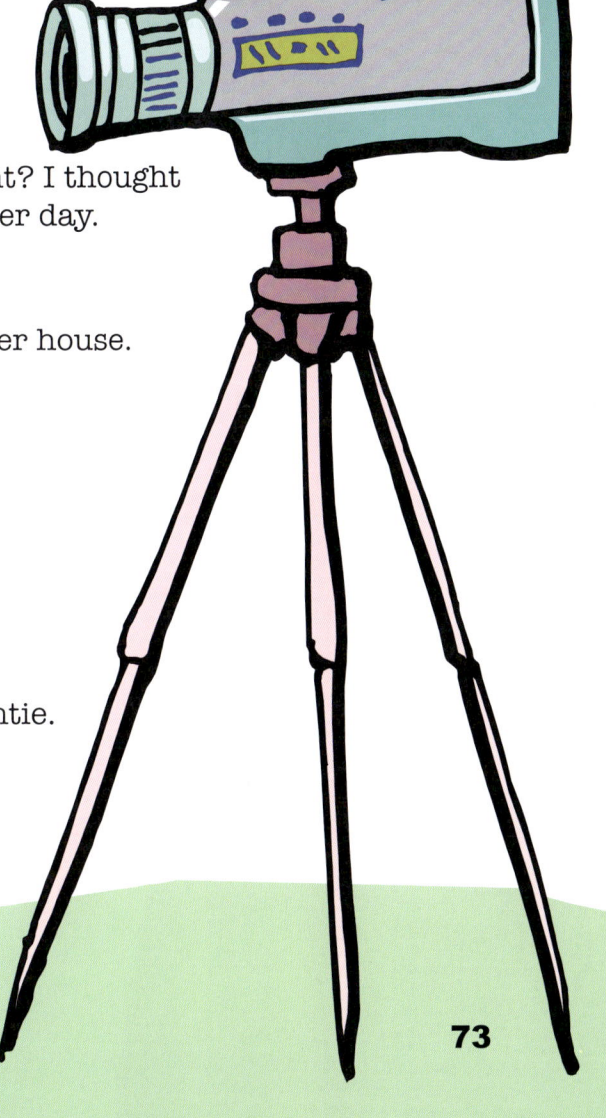

FOSTER MAMA
(hugs ANGIE)
Yes. I am your auntie, and Nicole is actually your cousin.

NICOLE
What?

FOSTER MAMA
You both know that Nicole's father was my brother, and I took her in when he died. But I never told you about Susan. I guess I was saving that information until you were older. Maybe I should have told you, but I thought it was too much for such a young soul.

ANGIE
(crying)
So why was I in a foster home for two years? Why did you take two years to come get me?

FOSTER MAMA

That's how long it took me to find you. Your mother didn't ever stay in one place for long. But I never stopped looking for you during those two years.

ANGIE

I'm so sorry! I promise never to do anything like this again. Don't let Nicole get in trouble for coming with me.

FOSTER MAMA

What do you mean, lovie? If I punish you, she'll just come and sit beside you, sharing your punishment. I know how you both are. You two are true sisters in every way that matters.

ANGIE

You and Nicole are the best things that ever happened to me. I guess I've been with my real family all along. From now on, I'll always be thankful for what I got.

Fade Out.

THE END

Mantack
The Wandering Wolf

by Rowan Thompson
with illustrations by M.Wolf

Chapter 1: Mantack

It was a dark night, and the wolves were roaming. The bravest of them all was named Mantack. She was a black wolf with golden eyes that shone brightly in the dark. Mantack spent her days wandering all over. This was her favorite pastime. One day while she was wandering, Mantack saw a small town with people who were moving around it busily. When Mantack looked closely, she saw two people from the town carrying a pole with two dead wolves hanging from it. Mantack knew who the wolves were. They were her parents!

"Oh, no!" Mantack howled, very scared and sad.

Suddenly, a person popped out from behind her. Mantack froze.

"Easy there! I'm not going to hurt you," said the stranger.

"Can I trust you?" Mantack asked, slowly turning around.

It was then that Mantack noticed that this person was not from the town! He was dressed differently.

"Yes, of course you can trust me! But how is it that you can speak? I did not think that wolves could really talk," the stranger said.

"I will tell you after you tell me your name," Mantack replied.

"My name is Silent Foot," said the man. "And your name is?"

"I am Mantack," said the wolf. "Why are you here?"

"I was looking for food for my tribe," Silent Foot said. Then he asked, "Why are you here?"

"I was wandering. I love to wander! Until I saw my parents hanging from that pole! They are dead!"

Silent Foot felt sorry for Mantack. He felt sad that Mantack's parents had been killed. Then Silent Foot had an idea.

"You can live with me and my tribe," said Silent Foot. "Or do you have somewhere else to go?"

"I don't have anywhere else to go," said the sad Mantack. "I would be happy to live with you and your tribe. I have only my brother, and I don't know where he is."

Chapter 2: Silent Foot's Village

On the way to Silent Foot's village, Mantack explained how she could talk.

"When I was a cub, my little brother and I were in the forest and found something strange that the humans had left behind. It looked odd, and we fell asleep after touching it. When we woke up, we had been changed. Talking was one of the changes, but that's all that I can remember of that day," said Mantack.

"What an interesting life you've had," said Silent Foot as they entered his village. People were hard at work in the village. When they arrived at Silent Foot's tepee, the chief welcomed them.

"Welcome back, Silent Foot," said the chief. "Who is your friend?"

Before Silent Foot could answer, Mantack said, "My name is Mantack."

"How can you speak?" said the chief in surprise.

"I don't know, but it seems that she has many gifts," Silent Foot answered.

"I will tell our people that we have a guest," the chief said. He turned and left the tepee without another word.

Silent Foot looked at Mantack crossly.

"I'm sorry," Mantack apologized. "I didn't mean to share my secret."

"It's all right," Silent Foot replied, seeming more at ease. "Just don't talk with the other villagers."

From that time on, when other people were around, Mantack spoke only as a wolf normally would, in yips and growls.

A few months later, the village was attacked.

"Run, Mantack!" Silent Foot yelled. "Run!"

"No! I won't leave you!" Mantack howled.

Just then, a blurry black object ran into Mantack. It grabbed hold of her and dragged her toward the forest.

"Let me go!" Mantack cried.

"I can't let you go," the black Blur said.

Mantack was too sad to notice that the Blur could talk. Later, in the dark forest, Mantack cried herself to sleep.

Chapter 3: The Identity of the Blur

When Mantack first woke up, she found herself in a cave. The cave was wide and filled with cobwebs. Mantack was about to leave the cave when she remembered the Blur. Curious about him, Mantack turned around and was shocked to see the Blur, right in front of her. She was even more shocked to realized that the Blur was her brother, Motiki.

"Motiki, is that you?" Mantack asked.

"Yes," Motiki replied.

"Your fur has changed. It used to be brown," Mantack said, as she kept glancing outside.

"The villagers painted it black so that I would look more like a village dog." Motiki replied, also looking outside.

It was a stormy day, with rain, thunder, and lightning. To Mantack and Motiki, the rain was not a bother. They thought it more of a melody than a noise.

"It's good to have you back," Mantack said softly.

Mantack and Motiki fell asleep, listening to the storm outside the cave.

Chapter 4: The Power of Mantack and Motiki

When the morning came and Mantack woke up once again, she wanted some fresh air. The ground outside the cave was very slippery and muddy. As Mantack walked to the mouth of the cave, she slipped on the wet mud and fell.

"Yip!" she cried aloud.

The sound of Mantack's cry echoed throughout the cave. Motiki woke up, hearing his sister's cry. As he came to the mouth of the cave to see what had happened, Mantack was standing there, covered in mud. Motiki laughed at the sight of Mantack, who looked so funny to him.

"Let's go to the river and clean you off," Motiki said, still chuckling.

After cleaning up, Mantack had an idea. "Let's go back to the village to see if Silent Foot is still alive," she said. "What do you think, Motiki?"

"I like it. Let's go!" replied Motiki.

Motiki led Mantack back to the village. When they arrived, the village was a wasteland. Everything was burned.

"Silent Foot!" Mantack cried.

"I'm over here!" Silent Foot cried from a distance.

Mantack and Motiki ran toward Silent Foot's voice. They found him stuck in between three dead horses.

"My brother and I will help you," Mantack said, relieved to see her friend.

"You found your brother?" Silent Foot said weakly.

"We will tell you everything after we get you out," Motiki said.

Mantack helped Motiki get the horses off Silent Foot, and then they helped him stand up.

"Now that you are free, we will tell you what happened," Mantack said.

Mantack and Motiki explained what had happened. After telling Silent Foot their story, they did not know what to do next.

"Now what?" Motiki asked.

"I want to see our home again," Mantack said. "After that we can start a new village."

"Let's go!" said Motiki.

So Silent Foot went with Mantack and Motiki to find their home. When they arrived there, the area was as plain as ever. All of a sudden, Motiki and Silent Foot were both caught in a large net.

"Help!" Silent Foot cried.

"Ha-ha-ha!" said a voice.

Mantack was the only one that was not in a net and could see that the voice belonged to a man. Mantack charged toward the man, who punched her in the face. Mantack flew to the ground.

"Is that the best you can do? Ha-ha-ha!" the man cried.

Mantack did not want to reveal her secret by talking, but she had something else on her mind. It was time to show one of her other powers. She was going to transform!

The man stepped forward. "I might take you with me in a net as I have done with your friends!"

"That is it!" Mantack thought. She pulled her fur back into her body. Black scales that shone blue in the sun replaced her fur and covered her entire body. And then Mantack grew five times her normal size, and her eyes began to glow as red as blood. Mantack was now a dragon!

"I'm in trouble!" shouted the man, frozen stiff with fear.

"Good idea, Sister," Motiki shouted. "I am going to transform, too!" When the man took his eyes off Mantack to glance at Motiki, he did not see a wolf.

He saw a bear! Motiki ripped through the net and landed right next to Mantack, the Dragon.

"We're going to take you down!" thought Mantack, as she stared at the man. Suddenly, the man let go of the rope that held Silent Foot in its netting. Silent Foot dropped, but Motiki caught him in his bearlike arms.

"Ahhhhhhhh! Help! Help!" cried the man, as he ran away.

Motiki placed Silent Foot down carefully on the ground. Slowly, Mantack and Motiki transformed back into wolves.

"That was really cool," said Silent Foot.

"Indeed, I think that is the second time that we have transformed," said Motiki.

"But how?" stammered Silent Foot.

Mantack and Motiki looked at each other.

"It's as I told you before," Mantack explained, "that something happened to us as cubs. Not only can we talk, but we can also transform!"

Mantack stopped, looking confused for a moment. "I still can't explain it," she said. "It's just something that we do."

There was a long uncomfortable silence.

"Well, do you want to make a new village?" asked Mantack, breaking the silence.

"Sure, why not?" Motiki said. "Silent Foot, how about looking for any villagers who remain, while Mantack and I look for wolves?"

"That is a good idea, Motiki," said Mantack. "Do you like his plan, Silent Foot?"

"I like it a lot. Let's split up," Silent Foot agreed.

Chapter 5: The New Village

Finding the stragglers took a long time. After months of searching, Mantack and Motiki came back with whatever wolves they could find, and Silent Foot came back with the remaining villagers. Building the new village was a lot of work. While the people made tepees, the wolves found hunting spots and food. By working together, they made a home for all. While the people hunted, the wolves guarded the village. In turn, the people provided warmth and shelter in harsh weather.

When Mantack grew up, she gave birth to two cubs with one of the wolves of the village. Their parents named them Silver Wind and Sunrise, but their stories are tales for another time.

Pieces of the Puzzle

by Tommie Sierra Middleton

The United States of America is often said to be the best country in the world. Where else can people who speak many different languages come and make a successful life for their families? Where else can people of different religions come and practice whatever religion they wish without being harmed? Where else could a little girl like me become a published author with the help of the world's greatest sorority, Alpha Kappa Alpha Sorority?

Last year, a 10-year-old girl named Rosa transferred to my class. Rosa was from Mexico and spoke very little English. I looked up her name and found that "Rosa" means "rose" in Spanish. I thought that talking about what our names mean would be a good way to begin to communicate with Rosa. My name is Tommie, which is a version of my father's name, Thomas. Then my cousin and I decided to teach English to Rosa. So we found Spanish-English dictionaries and Spanish books to help us. I believe that in this world, we need to help one another as much as we can.

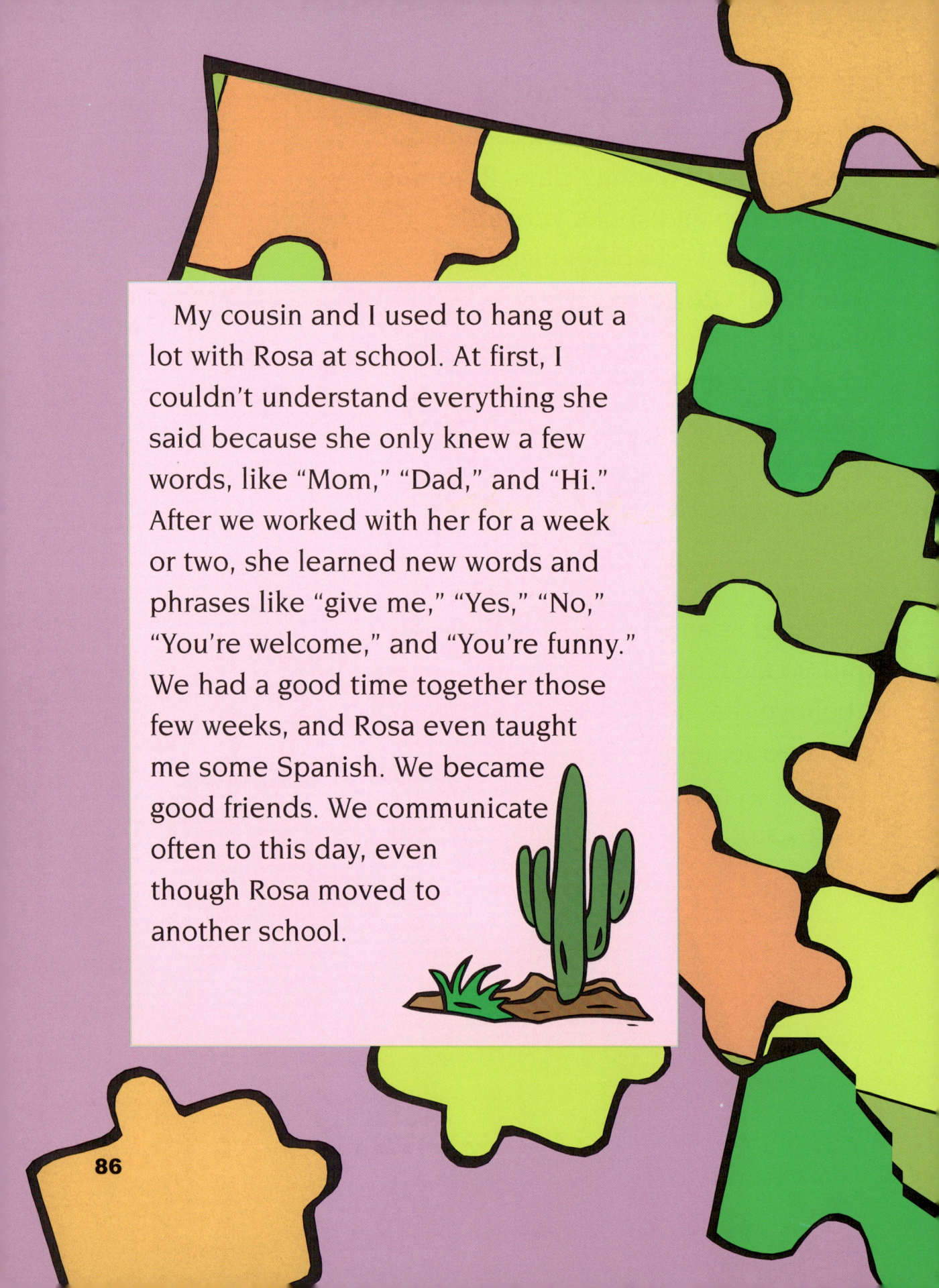

My cousin and I used to hang out a lot with Rosa at school. At first, I couldn't understand everything she said because she only knew a few words, like "Mom," "Dad," and "Hi." After we worked with her for a week or two, she learned new words and phrases like "give me," "Yes," "No," "You're welcome," and "You're funny." We had a good time together those few weeks, and Rosa even taught me some Spanish. We became good friends. We communicate often to this day, even though Rosa moved to another school.

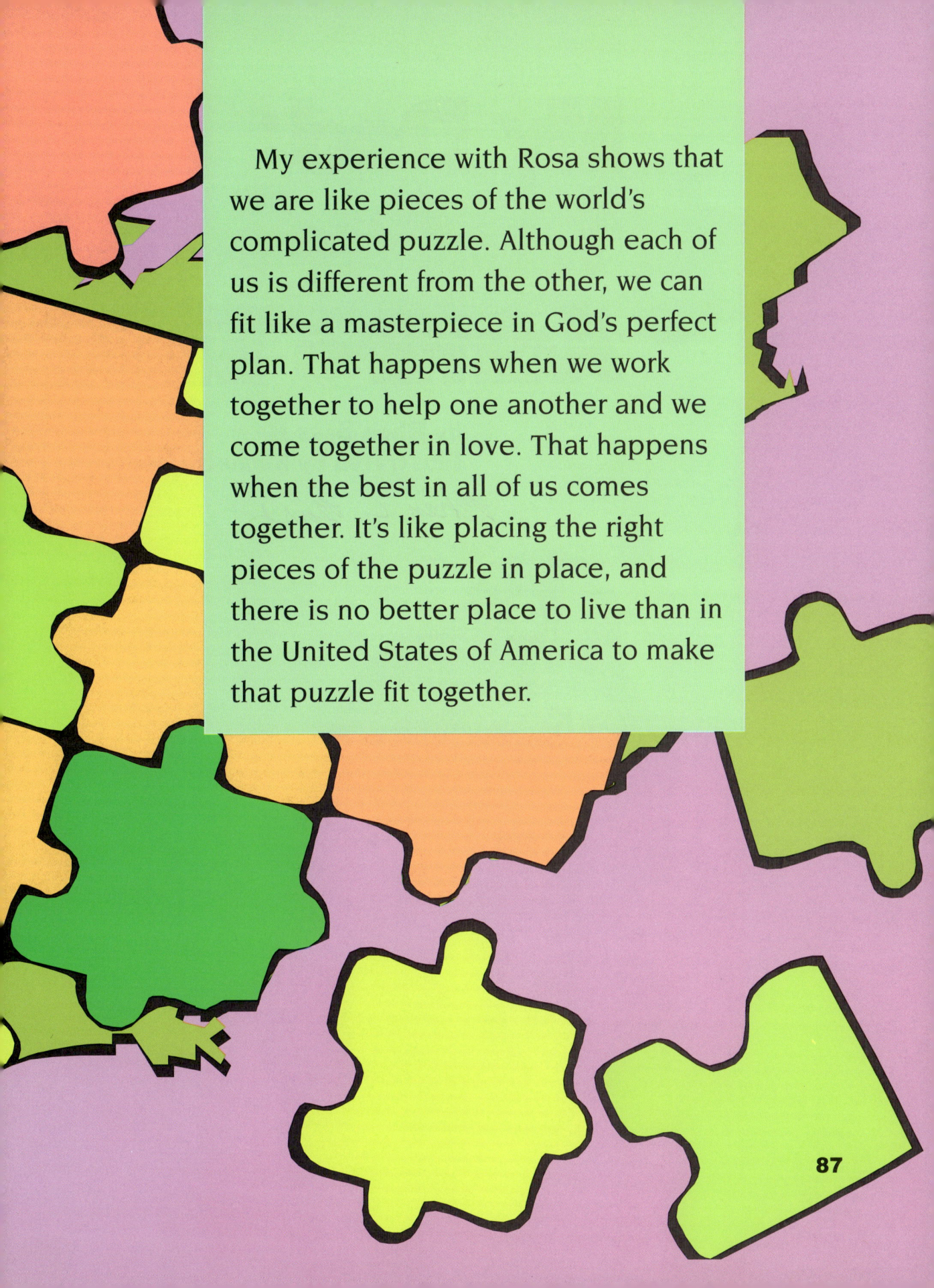

My experience with Rosa shows that we are like pieces of the world's complicated puzzle. Although each of us is different from the other, we can fit like a masterpiece in God's perfect plan. That happens when we work together to help one another and we come together in love. That happens when the best in all of us comes together. It's like placing the right pieces of the puzzle in place, and there is no better place to live than in the United States of America to make that puzzle fit together.

My Dad: The Person I Admire Most

by Rhen Bass II
Illustrated by Kenneth Flack

Some kids say they admire people with fame and fortune. For example, some people think highly of stars or celebrities such as Shaq, Barry Bonds, Beyoncé, and even Tiger Woods, to name a few. Do they really know these people? In fact, they only admire their fame and fortune. I took the time to really think about who I admire most. The person I came up with over and over again was my dad.

My dad has many good traits that make him the person I admire the most. My dad is so involved at my school that the other parents voted him Vice Chairman of the School Site Council. He is a PTA member and past treasurer. In fact, he was voted PTA Volunteer of the Year. He is recognized as a public speaker and teacher for Junior Achievement. He has even taught art in my class.

My dad often leaves work to come to my school to have lunch with me. He never leaves before playing a game of basketball with my friends and me. It is always my dad against all the kids. He lets the opposing team take many shots. Everyone knows that my dad is a great player. However, mysteriously, the kids' team wins every game.

Dad visits my school so much that the local newspaper wrote an article about his involvement. It was titled "PARENTS: Get Involved with Your Kids." It was written to encourage other parents to do the same. Most of my friends' dads seldom come to school. In addition, when they come they never stay for lunch or play at recess. Dad treats all the kids as if they are his own. They often race just to sit by him at the lunch table in the cafeteria. I have become the most popular kid on campus because of my dad's popularity at school. Kids admire me because of my dad's involvement. Boy, do I feel special. And it's all because of my dad.

When I was in the fifth grade, my dad was a chaperon on a field trip. Out of all the chaperons, he was the only dad. Our field trip included viewing an original copy of the Declaration of Independence at the main downtown Los Angeles Library. I had a great time, and having my dad there made it even better!

There is something else that is very significant about my dad, and that is that he is a great father. He always shows concern and compassion for my well-being. Whenever I have a scraped knee or a scratch, he puts a bandage on it to make it feel better. When I am sick and have to stay home from school, my dad stays home with me to cheer me up. He always makes me laugh when I'm down. He helps me with my homework and school projects, too.

My dad and I go to the movies together, attend the Lakers and Clippers basketball games, drive to see the San Diego Chargers football games, eat at nice restaurants, and visit other fun places.

My dad is an extremely hardworking and busy man. However, he always makes time for our family. Every day he drives about 25 miles to work. My dad is the CPA (Certified Public Accountant) and Vice President of Auditing at a large compensation insurance company.

My dad is also very involved with his fraternity. He holds positions on national and local levels and works closely with fraternity members at UCLA and the University of California Santa Barbara. His involvement with those young men increases my admiration for him. When I go to college, I want to be a Kappa just like my dad. My dad is in many organizations, and he is committed to every one of them.

Because of my parents' hard work, my dad has been able to take our family to many exciting places. We have been to many of the states in the United States, including Hawaii.

92

He has taken us to Canada, Washington, D.C., New York City, San Francisco, Orlando, San Diego, Detroit, Houston, San Antonio, Lake Tahoe, Las Vegas, Mexico, and many other places. During these trips, we visited many national monuments, historical attractions, and amusement parks. We also visited friends and relatives.

My dad has given me many gifts and presents. The gift I cherish most is my stuffed tiger that was given to me when I was born. When I was little, I named him Tiger. I would take Tiger on vacations and many other places to comfort me. When I was little, Tiger and I were inseparable. Now that I am older, I don't carry him around anymore, but every day when I come home from school, I'm glad to see Tiger's smiling face.

Another reason I admire my dad is that he is my Sunday school teacher. I love it when he teaches the lesson. Our class learns about the Bible with fun lessons, games, and activities, and we even receive prizes for participation.

It is nice to have someone who will love you, cherish you, care for you, and always "have your back." Now that is the essence of my dad. I feel blessed to have someone who will always love me, encourage me, and be my best friend. He was there when I was born and when I was sick, and he is someone who will always love me. For all these reasons, I can truly say the person I most admire is my Dad.

THE CLYDESDALE'S COURAGE

by Alexandra Bender

It was a day unlike any other day at Swiftly's Farm. You could hear the satisfying sound of the Clydesdale horses crunching oats and the clinking of hoofs meeting stone. In Stable Seven there was an excited gathering. A foal was being born.

This foal's name was Charm. His mother's name was Lucky. When he was only a day old, Charm learned how to walk. This was also his first day out of the stable at Swiftly's Farm. The summer heat warmed his silky coat. The tall grass moistened by the morning dew brushed his wobbly knees.

Charm started out with a trot and then progressed to a gallop. When it was time to go back to the stable, he did not follow orders and played hard to get. But he couldn't resist when someone came out with a large bucket of fresh oats. Off he galloped into the warmth of his new home, his stable.

As the year passed, the young Clydesdale grew loyal to his master. He earned his first pair of horseshoes. His master put the metal in the blazing fire, then plunged it in the cool water. Next, he nailed the metal shoe to Charm's hoof. Charm was as frightened as a deer running from the aim of a hunter.

One night, when the master was lighting the lantern in the horse stable, the hot match fell in the fresh hay and began to burn. Smoke filled the air. Suddenly, Charm woke up and started kicking the wall. He kicked and kicked and still there was no response. What could he do? The stable door was open, so he jumped out.

The blazing fire blocked the entrance. Charm knew he had to save his friends, but the sight of fire petrified him. He started walking backwards, and then a flame shot out. He was trapped, but he had to save his friends. Charm did not hesitate anymore; he made a run through the fire and out of the stable door. Off he ran to warn his master. The fire still raged.

There was no hope for the stable. The fire department arrived, but they were too late. There was nothing left of the building.

These days, Swiftly's stable is being rebuilt after the terrible fire. Sadly, Charm's mother, Lucky, passed away in the fire. But Charm saved twenty other horses that night. When Charm was jumping through the fire, he was burned on the stomach. This mark reminds people of who he is.

This is why Clydesdales represent courage. Courage means love and having the nerve to stand up to something that causes you to be afraid. The reason I know this is because I am Charm.

Me, Myself, and I

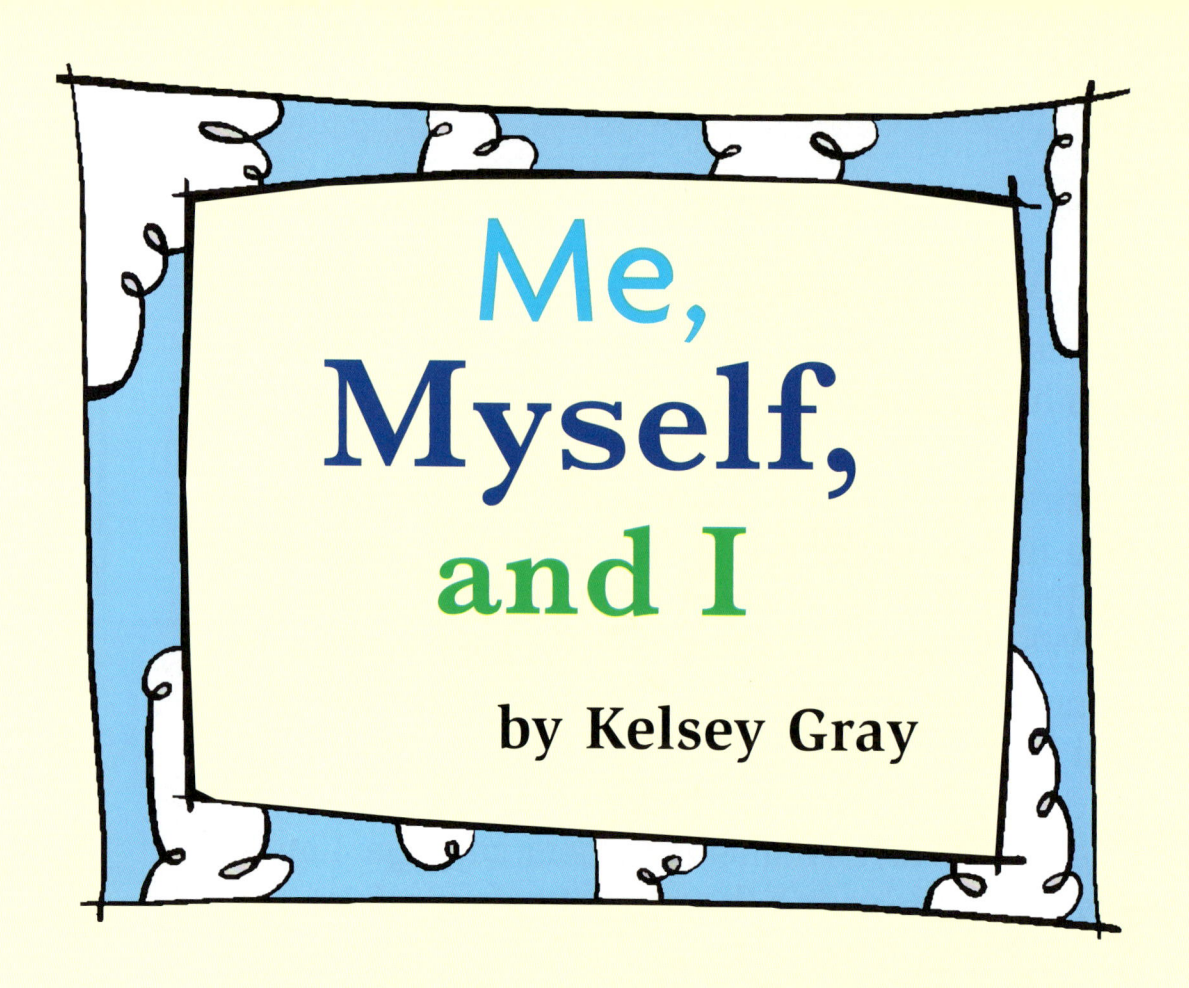

by Kelsey Gray

My life is mine, and your life is yours.
Don't try to change my life,
Except with good advice,
'Cause I am Me, Myself, and I.

The things I do only have to do with me.
The things you do have only to do with you.
Don't try to change my life,
Except with good advice,
'Cause I am Me, Myself, and I.

Be a leader and do the things you
 know are right.
I am sure others will follow
 your shining light.
Don't try to change my life,
Except with good advice,
'Cause I am Me, Myself, and I.

Hanging with the wrong crowd can get you caught up;
 drugs, gangs, and violence will get you locked up.
Don't try to change my life,
Except with good advice,
'Cause I am Me, Myself, and I.

Listen to your elders because they
   have been here long enough.
Thinking you're a know-it-all can
   be pretty tough.
Don't try to change my life,
Except with good advice,
'Cause I am Me, Myself, and I.

If you have friends and you are not
   treating them right,
They will find out that you are not
   showing your shining light.
Don't try to change my life,
Except with good advice,
'Cause I am Me, Myself, and I.

Being a friend means showing respect,
    loyalty, and trust.
Sometimes it even means arguing and
    a little fuss.
Don't try to change my life,
Except with good advice,
'Cause I am Me, Myself, and I.

Love one another through thick and
    through thin.
Best friends forever, always, until the end.
Don't try to change my life,
Except with good advice,
'Cause I am Me, Myself, and I.

Have faith in yourself and know
    you can do all things.
All things are possible if you just dream.
Don't try to change my life,
Except with good advice,
'Cause I am Me, Myself, and I.

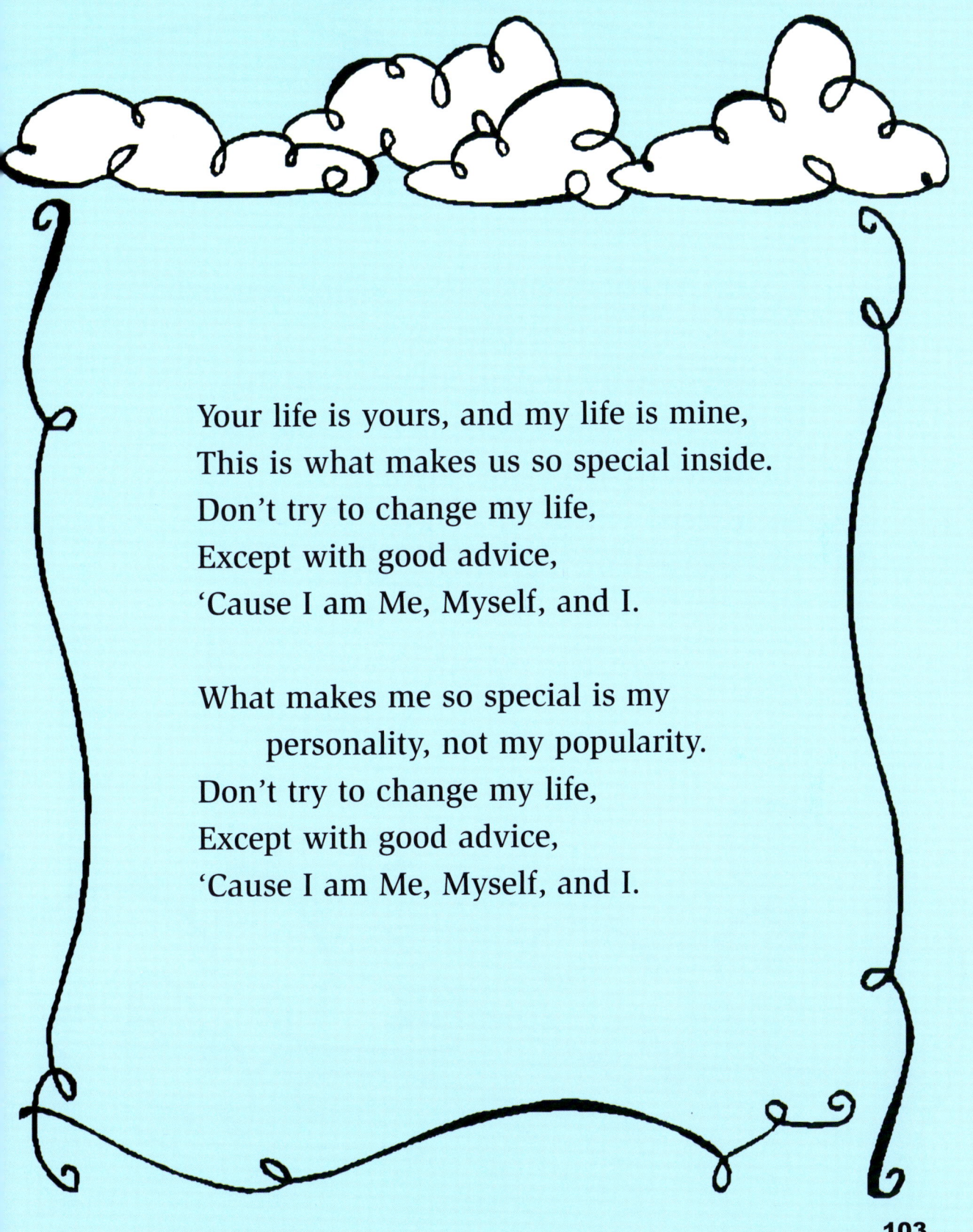

Your life is yours, and my life is mine,
This is what makes us so special inside.
Don't try to change my life,
Except with good advice,
'Cause I am Me, Myself, and I.

What makes me so special is my
personality, not my popularity.
Don't try to change my life,
Except with good advice,
'Cause I am Me, Myself, and I.

If you know someone is telling you right,
Listen and take that advice.
Tell it to all of your friends, and they
    will know what to do in the end.
Don't try to change my life,
Except with good advice,
'Cause I am Me, Myself, and I.

Being myself and doing the things
I know are right is what my life
    is all about.
I do not know about you,
But I know what I have to do.
Get my priorities in check
And live a life that's not a wreck.
Don't try to change my life,
Except with good advice,
'Cause I am Me, Myself, and I.

Now you know who I am and what
    I am about—
Determined to lead, staying focused,
And I will succeed.
Always remember and never forget.
Don't try to change my life,
'Cause I am, Me, Myself, and I!

My Most Unforgettable Experience

by Tabitha Ritchie

When I was three years old, I would spend most of my time watching TV and playing with my toys. My mother said I watched my Barney tapes over and over and never got tired of them. One day she decided to get me a surprise gift that would take my mind away from my Barney tapes and also be some company for me, as I was an only child. To my surprise, she brought home a puppy. My puppy was a very small dog with fluffy white hair. He had big eyes and a small nose. My mother said he was a Pekingese and that I could choose a name for him.

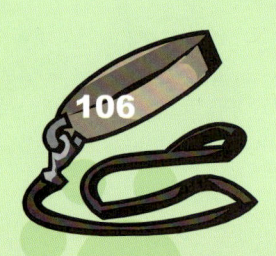

The first name that came to mind was "Fluffy," so that was what we called him. Fluffy was a house dog, so that meant he needed to be house trained. I needed to take him outside three times a day to do his business. I also fed him and bathed and played with him. He was like a brother to me. When I went to bed, he would sleep on the floor next to my bed. My mother said it was just as if she had another child. He needed to go to the veterinarian for his shots and heartworm pills. One day when my mom came to pick me up from school, she brought Fluffy into my classroom, and all my friends played with him. Ms. Newton and Mrs. Rolle, my teachers, patted him and said he was a pretty dog. Fluffy was really part of our family, and we always played together.

Fluffy also had a friend named Benji, a poodle. His owner was an 80-year-old lady by the name of Jeanne. Jeanne lived two doors down from us. When it was time to walk Benji, she would knock at our door, and we would walk our dogs together. We always took our pooper-scoopers with us and picked up the poop or covered it with sand so that it would not end up on someone's shoe. Just about every day for two years, we would walk and talk as we took our dogs out. We became very close.

One day we had to move from that address. We went to live in a duplex far away from Jeanne. This made me very sad. Fluffy was not happy there because it was near the road, so it was not safe to walk him. A decision had to be made about what to do with Fluffy. We were afraid because every time the door opened, he would run into the street. This was really not safe for him. My mom and dad made a decision and sat me down to break the bad news to me. They said because they did not want anything to happen to Fluffy, they would ask Jeanne if she could keep him. Jeanne was happy to take him because she said Benji was really missing Fluffy. She said that Benji was an old dog and she did not know how much longer he would be with her. The next day we packed Fluffy up, and he went to live with Jeanne. Jeanne treated Fluffy like her very own. We visited Fluffy and Jeanne mostly on the weekends, and he would always be so happy to see us.

One year later, Benji died. Jeanne was sad, but Fluffy was there to keep her company.

Eventually, our weekly visits turned into monthly ones. After a while, we visited only twice a year, on Halloween and on Christmas Day. As I was growing up and becoming interested in other things, I would think about Fluffy only once in a while. But sometimes I would show my friends pictures of all the fun Fluffy and I had together.

Six years passed, and I now had a sister, Tiffany, and a brother, T.J. They also visited Jeanne and Fluffy on Halloweens and Christmases with me and my parents.

One day about a month ago, we got a call from Jeanne's neighbor, Beth, who said that Jeanne had fallen and had broken her hip. Jeanne had to be taken to the hospital in Nassau. Beth asked if we would take care of Fluffy until Jeanne recovered and got out of the hospital. We were happy to do that. Jeanne had mentioned previously that if anything happened to her, she would want us to get Fluffy back. Jeanne was now 86 years old. When she came out of the hospital, she needed special care, and she had to go to a convalescent home for the aged. She said that she was being well taken care of there, and she was happy.

My family was happy to have Fluffy back with us. My sister and brother were adjusting to having him there, and they would play with him and chase him, and he would chase them.

Two weeks later we got a call from Beth, who said that Jeanne had died suddenly of a heart attack. We were very sad to hear that because we thought she was recovering and would be all right. There was a memorial service held for her at Restview Mortuary. She had no living family, but she had a lot of friends, and they all came out for the service. Her ashes were scattered on Xanadu Beach, where she used to walk with Fluffy occasionally.

Fluffy became sad for a couple of days, as if he knew Jeanne had died. He has now settled into our home and he is once again part of our family.

My experience in all of this was one that I would never forget. This is a story that I could tell my children and grandchildren. I learned that you never know what life has in store for you. I never thought that Fluffy would be back with us.

Yorktown's Lady Rattlesnakes

by Andrea Lloyd

It was championship season for basketball in Mississippi. The Yorktown High School Lady Rattlesnakes' basketball team was getting ready for their first game of the tournament. They had had a fun season because they had won all twelve of their regular season's games.

Yorktown is a busy little town of about 15,000 people located north of Jackson, the capital of Mississippi. The people of Yorktown love sports.

Yorktown High School sits right in the middle of town. The success of YHS's Lady Rattlesnakes had made the high school of 500 students and the town happy and proud, and excited that the girls had made it so far! Everyone planned to support the girls during the big tournament.

Dominique, Shaquara, Monique, and Jamie were all friends on the Lady Rattlesnake team. Jamie and Monique were sisters who had moved to Yorktown from New York two years before. Their cousin, who already went to Yorktown High School, had introduced the girls to Shaquara and Dominique. Jamie and Monique didn't like the other two girls at first, but when they discovered that Shaquara and Dominique liked basketball, they became best friends.

The Lady Rattlesnakes had been given the entire week off to practice for the weekend's championship tournament. The team would practice four times a day, with the first practice starting at 8 A.M. The first practice was for running and stretching. During the second they practiced lay-ups. At the third practice, they worked on three-point shots. At the end of the practice day, they put it all together in a practice game.

The day before the first game of the tournament, the girls were at their final practice at the gym. The team was out on the court practicing when Monique passed the ball to Jamie. Shaquara and Dominique had wanted the ball passed to them and when it wasn't, they just quit playing. The coach shouted to the girls to come over to her.

"Why did you stop playing in the middle of practice?" shouted the coach.

Shaquara answered, "Monique should have passed the ball to me, because I wanted to shoot."

"No, she should have passed it to me, because I would have made the shot!" Dominique said.

The coach told Monique to come over to where they were standing.

"Why didn't you pass to Shaquara or Dominique instead of Jamie?" asked the coach.

"Because they always get the ball, and Jamie was closest to the basket," Monique said.

"You were right, Monique. The important thing was that someone made the basket. Jamie was the closest one," said the coach.

The coach called over the entire team and said, "Girls, it doesn't matter who gets the ball. What's important is that you work together as a team. Really, no one player gets the points; the team gets the points, and wins or loses together."

Everyone shook hands and went back to practicing. The girls took the coach's advice and began to play as a team. They all made sure the ball was passed to the player in the best position to make the basket.

Finally, it was time for the Lady Rattlesnakes' first game of the championship. They had played this team three times before and beaten them every time. They did it again. That same day they had two more games…one team they had beaten twice during the season and another they had just beaten two weeks ago. They won easily against both teams.

Saturday was a cloudy day with thunderstorms. One of the Lady Rattlesnakes' games was canceled because a team's bus got stuck in the mud. This meant the team only had one game on Saturday and would have two on Sunday if they won on Saturday.

The Lady Anacondas were from Belmont, Mississippi. Like the Lady Rattlesnakes, they had gone undefeated all season. The Anacondas were known for their tricky court play. The Lady Rattlesnakes were ready. With just five seconds left to play in the game, the score was 80 for the Rattlesnakes and 78 for the Anacondas. The Lady Anacondas had the ball, but when they took the shot, it bounced off the rim, and the Lady Rattlesnakes won. They were still undefeated.

It was early Sunday morning when the Lady Rattlesnakes went to the gym again. They were going to get one practice in before the last two games. During the practice Shaquara slipped on the floor and broke her wrist. Everyone on the team was upset.

The coach said, "We've made it this far. You will have to go on and play without her. Remember you are a team. You work together!"

The first game on Sunday was no problem. The Lady Rattlesnakes won 50 to 26. The final game was for the state championship against the Lady Alligators of Pittsburg, Mississippi. All of Yorktown was at this game, happy the girls had made it to the finals.

The team was concerned they were playing without Shaquara, but the players remembered what the coach had said. This game was really hard for the girls because the Lady Alligators were doing two plays at once. They got out to a 14-point lead in the second quarter, so the Lady Rattlesnakes decided to do three plays at a time. They confused the Lady Alligators so much that the Gators didn't score a point in the third quarter. The game ended with a final score of 80 for the Lady Rattlesnakes and 70 for the Lady Alligators.

Everyone who had been pulling for the Lady Rattlesnakes ran out on the court yelling and cheering. The team accepted the state championship trophy proudly. Then the coach said, "I repeat…teamwork has brought you this far!" The team agreed and took a victory lap around the gym.

Spring Makes Me Feel...

by Jordan Wynn

I like spring, yes I do. I like spring, how about you? Spring is the time of year when all of our senses are heightened. Spring is the time of year when everything just tastes better, smells better, appears brighter and clearer, and feels smoother and gentler to the touch.

I like springtime, first of all, because it is the season that is closest to summer. Summer is the best season of the year, because school is out. I recognize that in order to enjoy summer, I must first have a spring. Spring prepares us for the summer.

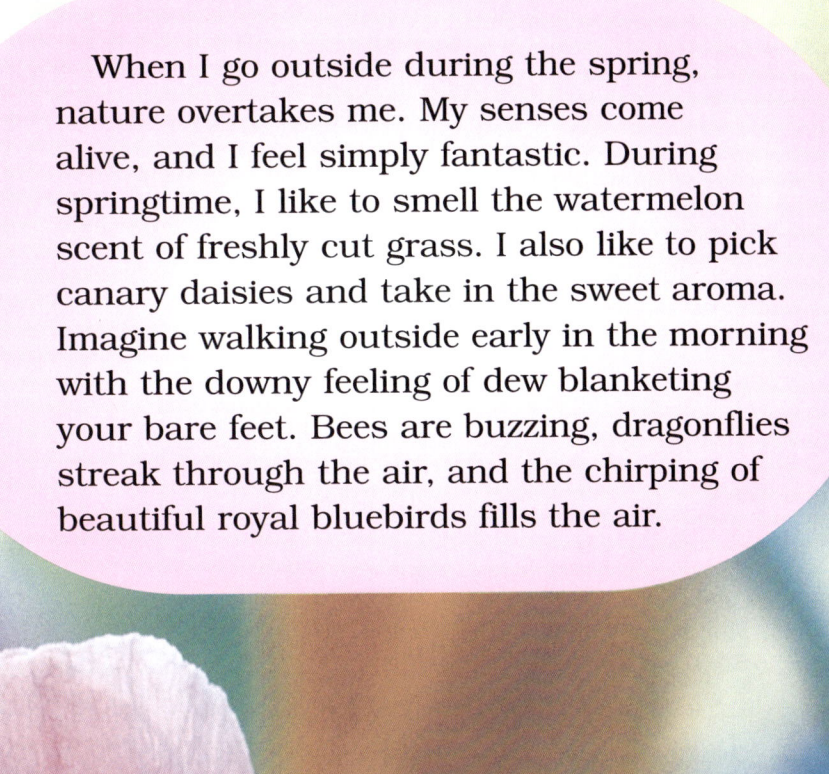

When I go outside during the spring, nature overtakes me. My senses come alive, and I feel simply fantastic. During springtime, I like to smell the watermelon scent of freshly cut grass. I also like to pick canary daisies and take in the sweet aroma. Imagine walking outside early in the morning with the downy feeling of dew blanketing your bare feet. Bees are buzzing, dragonflies streak through the air, and the chirping of beautiful royal bluebirds fills the air.

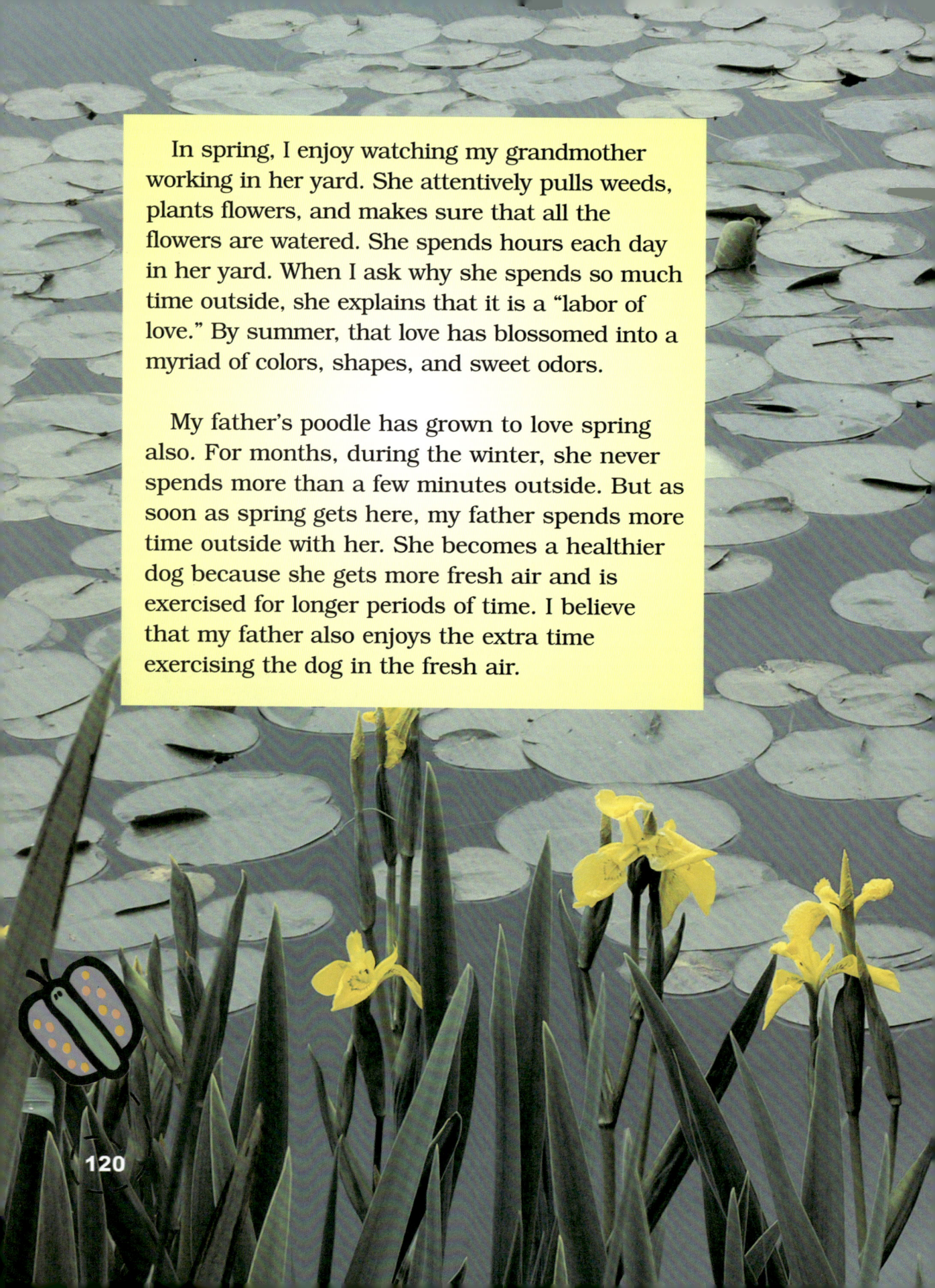

In spring, I enjoy watching my grandmother working in her yard. She attentively pulls weeds, plants flowers, and makes sure that all the flowers are watered. She spends hours each day in her yard. When I ask why she spends so much time outside, she explains that it is a "labor of love." By summer, that love has blossomed into a myriad of colors, shapes, and sweet odors.

My father's poodle has grown to love spring also. For months, during the winter, she never spends more than a few minutes outside. But as soon as spring gets here, my father spends more time outside with her. She becomes a healthier dog because she gets more fresh air and is exercised for longer periods of time. I believe that my father also enjoys the extra time exercising the dog in the fresh air.

My taste buds have also grown to love springtime. Just imagine the taste of finger-licking good barbecue sauce. The first ribs of the season are juicier, more tender, and more mouthwatering than those we eat later in the summer. Spring also brings my tiger-blood snow cone. Ah—the sweet taste of juice and ice in a refreshing snow cone.

The sensational springtime breeze on my face takes me to faraway places—Bermuda, the Bahamas, or Cozumel. It is as gentle as my mother's hand gently placed upon my face, as smooth as watching graceful dolphins swimming in sparkling blue ocean water. Another beauty of nature that springtime brings is the weather.

It's not too hot or too cold. The sun shines just brightly enough. And while pollen may affect some people, it is just a part of nature coming alive during this magnificent time of year.

I like spring, yes I do. I like spring, how about you?

Young Author Biographies

Rhen Bass II attends Sycamore Canyon School in California. He loves English and science classes. Rhen likes to swim, run track, and ride his bike. He also enjoys reading books, and he recommends Avi's novel *Don't You Know There's a War On?* Rhen finds that writing helps him to express himself, and in taking part in the Young Authors Program, he discovered that sticking to something makes good things happen.
Sponsoring Chapter: Xi Kappa Omega, Oxnard, California

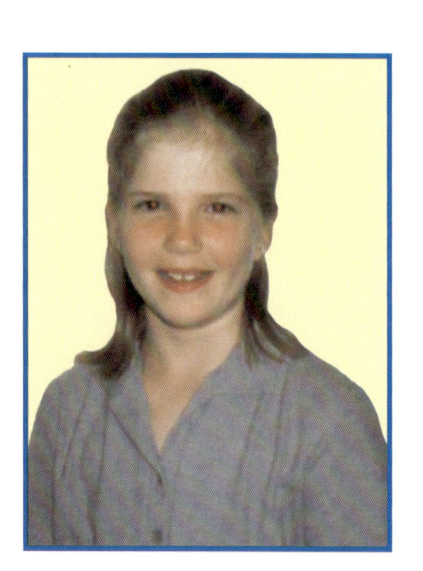

Alexandra Bender enjoys school life at Fairlawn Elementary School in Virginia. Her favorite subject is writing, because, as she says, there are no fences to the creativity and adventure in writing. Other things she enjoys doing are drawing, spending time with her friends, and reading books such as *The Lion, the Witch, and the Wardrobe* and the other Narnia books by C.S. Lewis. She says that her three favorite things are action, adventure, and animals.
Sponsoring Chapter: Upsilon Omicron Omega, Norfolk, Virginia

Ashley Buckner is a student at Lucy D. Slowe Elementary School. Her favorite subjects are math and science. She spends a lot of her spare time reading. Ashley is one of the many fans of the Harry Potter series and hopes that J.K. Rowling finishes the final book soon. She likes expressing realistic feelings in her writing, and she feels that the Young Authors Program has helped her learn more about editing her work.
Sponsoring Chapter: Xi Zeta Omega, Washington, D.C.

Kelsey Gray attends Southwind Middle School in Tennessee. There her favorite subject is social studies. She leads a busy life playing soccer and taking part in Girl Scout activities. The book Kelsey likes best is *Because of Winn-Dixie* by Kate DiCamillo. As a Young Author, Kelsey thinks that the most important thing she has learned is that a good writer should always try to grab readers' attention quickly.
Sponsoring Chapter: Phi Lambda Omega, Memphis, Tennessee

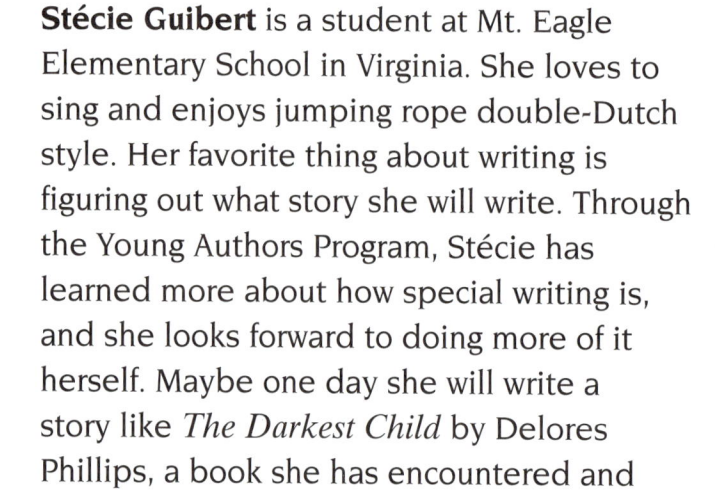

Stécie Guibert is a student at Mt. Eagle Elementary School in Virginia. She loves to sing and enjoys jumping rope double-Dutch style. Her favorite thing about writing is figuring out what story she will write. Through the Young Authors Program, Stécie has learned more about how special writing is, and she looks forward to doing more of it herself. Maybe one day she will write a story like *The Darkest Child* by Delores Phillips, a book she has encountered and been amazed by.
Sponsoring Chapter: Lambda Kappa Omega, Fairfax, Virginia

Peyton Hawkins goes to E.T. Hamilton Elementary School in New Jersey, where her favorite subjects are math and science. She absolutely loves animals and hopes one day to become a veterinarian. She also enjoys spending time with her friends, playing soccer, and telling jokes to her grandmother. As an avid reader, Peyton recommends *Redwall* by Brian Jacques, the first book in an exciting series about animals. In her writing, Peyton frequently tells stories about her family.
Sponsoring Chapter: Theta Pi Omega, Willingboro, New Jersey

Sh'Zavia Hill is a student at Cobb Elementary School in Alabama, where she especially enjoys math. When she isn't doing schoolwork, she enjoys settling in with a good book. The many books from the Sweet Valley Twins series by Francine Pascal are favorites of hers. She has discovered that making up her own stories can be even more fun than reading books by other authors. Sh'Zavia's favorite thing to write is poetry.
Sponsoring Chapter: Iota Mu Omega, Anniston, Alabama

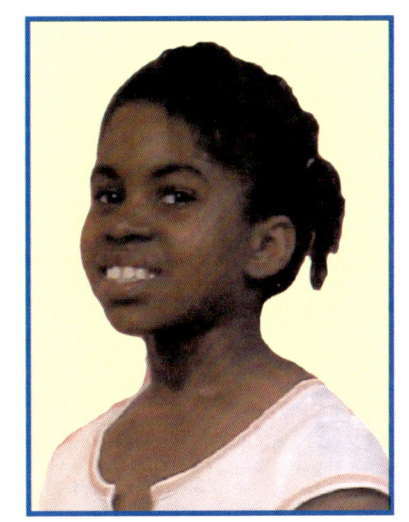

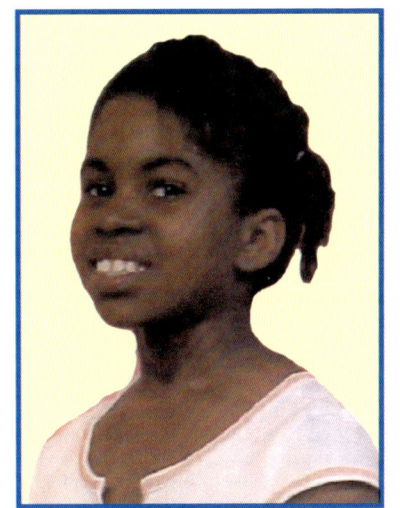

Rakia Levesque goes to West Elementary School in Ohio. She especially enjoys learning math. In her spare time, she enjoys being with her family and friends, skating, and dancing. She likes reading books, and one book she especially recommends is *Pass It On: African American Poetry for Children*, edited by Wade Hudson. The Young Authors Program has taught Rakia that you never know how far your imagination can go until you try.
Sponsoring Chapter: Epsilon Mu Omega, Youngstown, Ohio

Andrea Lloyd goes to the Mississippi School for the Blind, where her favorite subject is math. She excels in basketball and other sports. In her free time, Andrea enjoys talking to her friends, listening to music, dancing, and reading books such as *A Series of Unfortunate Events*, the popular series by Lemony Snicket and Brett Helquist. Andrea finds the stories she reads to be a great inspiration for her own writing.

ZaKiria Mays spends her weekdays at Atkinson Elementary School in Georgia. She enjoys reading both in class and in her spare time. A favorite book of hers is *Katie Kazoo, Switcheroo: Who's Afraid of Fourth Grade* by Nancy E. Krulik. ZaKiria would like to become an author one day. She is thankful for the encouragement that the Young Authors Program gave her to continue writing.
Sponsoring Chapter: Xi Beta Omega, Griffin, Georgia

Tommie Sierra Middleton, who goes to A.C. Corcoran Elementary School in South Carolina, enjoys both math and social studies. She also likes to draw, practice the piano, play sports, and sing. This avid reader loves the Harry Potter books and can't wait for the next installment to come out. When she writes, she loves to express herself and use her imagination. Through the Young Authors Program, she learned that little girls can be successful writers just as adults can.
Sponsoring Chapter: Omicron Rho Omega, North Charleston, South Carolina

Kristen Pratt attends Sadie Curtis Primary School in the Bahamas, where she enjoys math and being helpful to the teacher. Kristen enjoys traveling and writing stories about places and people. From the Young Authors Program, Kristen learned that writing stories is not only fun but important. She encourages other children to take part in the program. Kristen takes pride in doing well at school, and her wish is for all her readers to do well at school also.
Sponsoring Chapter: Eta Psi Omega, Nassau, Bahamas

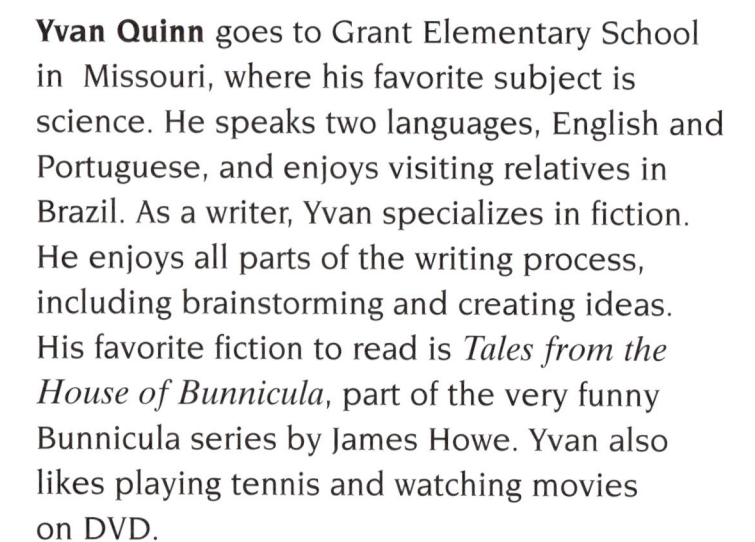

Yvan Quinn goes to Grant Elementary School in Missouri, where his favorite subject is science. He speaks two languages, English and Portuguese, and enjoys visiting relatives in Brazil. As a writer, Yvan specializes in fiction. He enjoys all parts of the writing process, including brainstorming and creating ideas. His favorite fiction to read is *Tales from the House of Bunnicula*, part of the very funny Bunnicula series by James Howe. Yvan also likes playing tennis and watching movies on DVD.
Sponsoring Chapter: Kappa Chi Omega, Columbia, Missouri

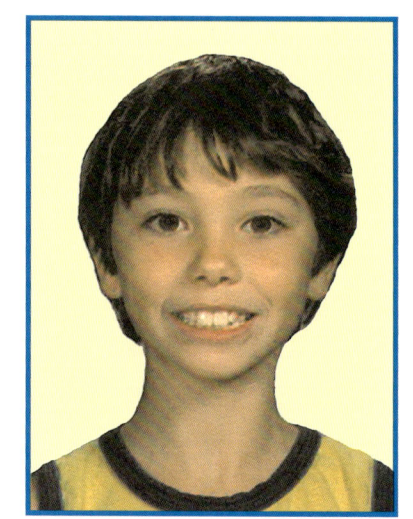

Tabitha Ritchie goes to Mary Star of the Sea Catholic School in the Bahamas. Math is her favorite subject. For fun, she writes poetry and stories, especially funny ones. Fluffy, the dog in her story in this anthology, is her real dog, and she enjoyed making him the main character of a story. She is grateful to the Young Authors Program for giving her the chance to do so.
Sponsoring Chapter: Pi Upsilon Omega, Freeport, Grand Bahama Island

Azuré Smith is a student at Julia C. Frazier Elementary School in Texas. There, she enjoys science and math. She loves taking books out of the library and recommends *Amelia Writes Again* by Marissa Moss. The Young Authors Program has shown Azuré that writing can be fun, because a writer can express her own ideas and create new characters. Her long-term goals include becoming a pediatrician and being elected the first woman president of the United States.
Sponsoring Chapter: Omicron Mu Omega, Dallas, Texas

Chanel Smith enjoys learning math at Trinity Lutheran School in California. She loves reading the Junie B. Jones books by Barbara Park, including *Junie B. Jones Is a Party Animal*. Chanel likes writing because it can show the author's feelings about a subject. As she participated in the Young Authors Program, she learned how to be comfortable sharing her feelings about a subject very precious to her, her grandmother.
Sponsoring Chapter: Theta Alpha Omega, Long Beach, California

MyKayla Strother is a student at Douglas Alternative Elementary School in Ohio. She likes both reading and math. She feels that taking part in the Young Authors Program has allowed her to learn more about how important and satisfying writing is. Along with writing, MiKayla enjoys drawing, spending time with her friends, and reading books. Her favorite story character by another author is Junie B. Jones, from the series by Barbara Park.
Sponsoring Chapter: Alpha Sigma Omega, Columbus, Ohio

Rowan Thompson goes to Ponderosa Elementary School in Colorado. There, she enjoys reading both in the classroom and for enjoyment. Her favorite book is the fantasy *Dragon Rider* by Cornelia Funke. Fantasy is a kind of literature that Rowan also enjoys writing. She feels that writing is a great outlet for the imagination and has enjoyed taking part in the Young Authors Program.
Sponsoring Chapter: Mu Omega Omega, Aurora, Colorado

Starre Williams attends Washington School in Illinois. Her favorite subject is math. She enjoys being a part of her community and helping others around the neighborhood. Other things she likes to do are swimming, dancing, jumping rope double-Dutch style, and reading books. One book she has liked is Lurlene McDaniel's *The Girl Death Left Behind*. To Starre, writing gives an author the opportunity to express feelings that could happen in everyday life.
Sponsoring Chapter: Nu Omicron Omega, Springfield, Illinois

Lisa Wilson is a student at Ethel Hedgeman Lyle Academy in Missouri. There, she especially enjoys language arts. When she has spare time, she likes to play traditional games such as Connect Four. She also loves to write, which she feels gives her the chance to be creative. Through the Young Authors Program, Lisa was happy to learn all the steps that a good author goes through to refine and present a story to readers. Lisa is fond of books from the Goosebumps series by R.L. Stine, including *My Best Friend Is Invisible*.
Sponsoring Chapter: Omicron Theta Omega, St. Louis, Missouri

Jordan Wynn attends Grambling Middle Magnet School, where she enjoys both science and English. She loves to write poetry and spend time with her family and also enjoys traveling. Her favorite thing about writing is coming up with adventurous ideas, and she feels that the Young Authors Program has taught her more about the writing process. A book Jordan enjoys is *The Pigman* by Paul Zindel.
Sponsoring Chapter: Epsilon Psi Omega, Grambling, Louisiana

Alpha Kappa Alpha Sorority, Incorporated
Young Authors Honorable Mention by Region
Grades 2–3

North Atlantic
Junius Onome Williams "Walk to the Light"
Omicron Xi Omega
Montclair, New Jersey

Mid-Atlantic
Bryana Robles "The Person I Admire Most"
Lambda Omega
Newport News, Virginia

South Atlantic
Xaykevia Stribling "The Pencil That Almost Changed My Life"
Gamma Theta Omega
Tampa, Florida

Great Lakes
QuiNae Slater "A Surprise for Wilbert"
Eta Iota Omega
Inkster, Michigan

South Eastern
Jalen Jones "Who Can Be a Hero"
Beta Nu Omega
Montgomery, Alabama

South Central
Silvia Pera "The Key Sword"
Chi Omicron Omega
Katy, Texas

Central
Calone Jones "The Courage to Be Me"
Epsilon Kappa Omega
Milwaukee, Wisconsin

Mid-Western
Amber Santiago

"The Princess and the Dragon"
Mu Omega Omega
Aurora, Colorado

Far Western
Rachel Janel Richardson

"A Princess Story"
Xi Kappa Omega
Oxnard, California

International
Daniel Koch

"My Most Unforgettable Experience"
Rho Nu Omega
Seoul, Korea

Young Authors Honorable Mention by Region
Grades 4–6

North Atlantic
China Owens

"Misaki, Earth's Hero"
Upsilon Delta Omega
Cherry Hill, New Jersey

Mid-Atlantic
Tanya Renee Freeman

"Why?"
Gamma Upsilon Omega
Hampton, Virginia

South Atlantic
Trelvonta Peeples

"The Person I Admire Most"
Nu Tau Omega
Denmark, South Carolina

Great Lakes
Shaquille Turner

"Sunday Dinner"
Delta Nu Omega
Rochester, New York

South Eastern
Devonte Powell

"The Passion of Freedom"
Nu Kappa Omega
Clarksville, Tennessee

South Central
Tyroné Hawkins

"Because I Am Black—My Story"
Nu Gamma Omega
Baton Rouge, Louisiana

Central
Ariel Briana Jordan

"Representing My Mother"
Chi Sigma Omega
Bolingbrook, Illinois

Mid-Western
Kendull Anderson

"The Sunset of My Mother's Life"
Theta Upsilon Omega
Lawton, Oklahoma

Far Western
Tatiana Hayes

"The Best of Friends"
Epsilon Xi Omega
San Diego, California

International
Stefanny Sanchez

"Viendo Mas Alla—Looking Beyond"
Sigma Xi Omega
Bermuda

Mississippi School for the Blind
Bridget Harkins

"My New Shoes"

National Judges

Donna Elam, Ed.D.
Vice Chair, Florida Commission on Human Relations
Associate Director, Southeastern Equity Center

Valada Flewellyn
Poet and Storyteller
Poet Laureate, Jack and Jill of America

Adria Klein, Ph.D.
Professor Emeritus, California State University,
    San Bernardino
Reading Hall of Fame Inductee
Member, Board of Directors, 1997–2000,
    International Reading Association

Jason Powe
General Editor of the Anthology

Reginald L. Powe
Founder, Metropolitan Teaching and Learning Company

Regional Judges

North Atlantic Region

Len McNair
U.S. Army (Retired)

Judith Panicucci
Educator

Dehlia Jenkins
Educator

George Gardner
Grant Writer

Jerry Webster, Ph.D.
Educator

Mid-Atlantic Region

Terry D'Italia
Director of Communications
and Public Information Officer

Jackie Hardy
Senior Director, Parent and
Community Involvement

John Motley
Executive Director, External Affairs

John Sims
Supervisor, Corporate Security

South Atlantic Region

Dorothy C. Young
Retired Elementary Educator

Dr. Mary L. Cassidy
Professor, South Carolina State
University

Vernitta Tucker
High School English Teacher

Mary Amos
High School Teacher

Joesph R. Lefft, Esquire
Law School Professor, Entrepreneur

Teresa Anderson
High School Teacher

Great Lakes Region

David Lawrence
Teacher, Meadowdale High School
Dayton Public School System

137

Darlene Mathews
Manager, Labor Relations
DaimlerChrysler Corporation

Cordelia Penn
Retired Elementary Teacher
Dayton Public School System

LaDawn Prosser
General Supervisor
Delphi Corporation

Ann Robinson
Administrator, Accounting
Jewish Federation

South Eastern Region
Jean Linton
Retired Educator

Catherine Torrence
Retired Educator

Emily Washington
Retired Educator

South Central Region
Pamela Brown
Former Librarian of the Year
Dallas Independent School District

Bridgette Carraway
Teacher
Dallas Independent School District

Freddie Ransom
Master Reading Teacher, Grant Writer
Dallas Independent School District

Don A. Williams
Retired Administrator
Dallas Independent School District

Sandra Willis
Teacher
Dallas Independent School District

Central Region
Louise Berland, Ph.D.
College Professor

Karen O'Donnell, Ed.D.
College Professor

Elizabeth Nakamura
High School English Teacher

Darlene Richardson, Ph.D.
College Professor

Steve Nash, Ed.D.
College Professor

Mid-Western Region

Sherri Langston
Certified Insurance Plan Builder

Cindy Hombs
Senior Medical Underwriter

Frankie Buckley-Lewis
Manager, Senior Living

Far Western Region

Irvin Jefferson
Coordinator of Prevention and Student Services
Lodi Unified School District

Vanessa Smith-Studky
Vice Principal, Delta Sierra Middle School
Lodi Unified School District

Debrae Bownes
Clerk, Christa McAuliffe Middle School
Lodi Unified School District

International Region

Michelle Beresford
School Librarian

Andrea Grant
Patient Advocate

**Alpha Kappa Alpha Sorority, Incorporated
National Program Committee
Extends Appreciation to the Following Partners
for Their Support**

**Ivy Reading AKAdemy
and Young Author Partners**

United States Department
of Education
Former U.S. Secretary of Education
Rod Paige

Creative Curriculum Initiatives
Reginald Powe

Merrill Lynch
Dr. Eddy Bayardelle
www.ml.com

DaimlerChrysler

**Partners/The Black Family
and Health Initiatives**

The Points of Light Foundation
Dr. Robert Goodwin, CEO
www.pointsoflight.org

National Institute of Child
Health and Human Development
National Institutes of Health
Dr. Yvonne T. Maddox,
Deputy Director

Partners/Economic Initiatives

KPMG Ph.D. Project
Bernie Milano
www.kpmgfoundation.org

Alpha Kappa Alpha Sorority, Incorporated: Who We Are

Founded in 1908, Alpha Kappa Alpha Sorority became America's first Greek-letter organization established by Black college women. Headquartered in Chicago, Illinois, the organization today thrives as a sisterhood of college-educated women who have chosen this affiliation as a means of self-fulfillment through volunteer service. AKA cultivates and encourages high scholastic and ethical standards; promotes unity and friendship among college women; alleviates problems concerning girls and women; maintains a progressive interest in college life; and serves all mankind through a nucleus of more than 170,000 women in the United States, the Caribbean, Europe, and Africa.

The 2002–2006 theme is "The Spirit of Alpha Kappa Alpha." Program targets include Education, the Black Family, Health, Economics, and the Arts. During this four-year period, Alpha Kappa Alpha provided more than four million hours of volunteer services and $22 million to support service projects across the country. These projects benefited 18.6 million people.

In education, the Ivy Reading AKAdemy initiative has a three-year grant of $1.5 million awarded by the U.S. Department of Education to provide one-on-one tutoring in reading for at-risk children (K–3). AKA also sponsors the Young Authors Program and the Presidential Freedom Scholarship Program.

"Within the Black Family" is our National Family Volunteer Day. Our members join with the Points of Light Foundation the third Saturday in November to help raise awareness of the importance of family volunteering.

In the health area, our chapters focus on cancer awareness, diabetes, cardiovascular health, sickle cell anemia, and HIV/AIDS awareness, as well as a Buckle Up initiative with the U.S. Department of Transportation. In partnership with the National Institute of Child Health and Human Development of the National Institutes of Health, AKA promotes awareness of risk reduction strategies for Sudden Infant Death Syndrome (SIDS).

The sorority also partners with Merrill Lynch to focus on youth financial literacy; Tyson Foods, who has sponsored our Leadership Fellows Program for the past three years; the American Cancer Society; DaimlerChrysler; Creative Curriculum Initiatives; and KPMG, to name just a few.

For more information on AKA, go to **www.aka1908.com**.

Index of Authors

Bass, Rhen, 88, 122
Bender, Alexandra, 94, 122
Buckner, Ashley, 62, 123
Gray, Kelsey, 98, 123
Guibert, Stécie, 14, 124
Hawkins, Peyton, 24, 124
Hill, Sh'Zavia, 12, 125
Levesque, Rakia, 56, 125
Lloyd, Andrea, 112, 126
Mays, ZaKiria, 18, 126
Middleton, Tommie Sierra, 84, 127
Pratt, Kristen, 38, 127
Quinn, Yvan, 42, 128
Ritchie, Tabitha, 106, 128
Smith, Azuré, 28, 129
Smith, Chanel, 34, 129
Strother, MyKayla, 46, 130
Thompson, Rowan, 76, 130
Williams, Starre, 68, 131
Wilson, Lisa, 50, 131
Wynn, Jordan 118, 132